my revision notes

OCR AS
RELIGIOUS STUDIES
RELIGIOUS ETHICS

Jill Oliphant

HODDER
EDUCATION

Acknowledgements

Thanks to OCR for permission to reproduce the Mark Scheme on page 7, taken from Unit G572, June 2011, www.ocr.org.uk.

Exam practice questions © OCR G572 2007–2012. Answer guidance (online) has not been written or approved by OCR.

Every effort has been made to trace all copyright holders, but if any have been inadvertently overlooked the Publishers will be pleased to make the necessary arrangements at the first opportunity.

Although every effort has been made to ensure that website addresses are correct at time of going to press, Hodder Education cannot be held responsible for the content of any website mentioned in this book. It is sometimes possible to find a relocated web page by typing in the address of the home page for a website in the URL window of your browser.

Hachette UK's policy is to use papers that are natural, renewable and recyclable products and made from wood grown in sustainable forests. The logging and manufacturing processes are expected to conform to the environmental regulations of the country of origin.

Orders

Please contact Bookpoint Ltd, 130 Milton Park, Abingdon, Oxon OX14 4SB.
Telephone: +44 (0)1235 827720.
Fax: +44 (0)1235 400454.
Lines are open 9.00a.m.–5.00p.m., Monday to Saturday, with a 24-hour message answering service. Visit our website at www.hoddereducation.co.uk

First published in 2013 by
Hodder Education,
An Hachette UK Company
338 Euston Road
London NW1 3BH

Impression number 10 9 8 7 6 5
Year 2017 2016 2015

Cover photo © porcorex/iStockphoto

Typeset in CronosPro-Lt 12pts by Datapage (India) Pvt. Ltd.
Printed in Spain

A catalogue record for this title is available from the British Library
ISBN 978 14441 82491

Get the most from this book

Everyone has to decide his or her own revision strategy, but it is essential to review your work, learn it and test your understanding. The Revision Notes will help you to do that in a planned way, topic by topic. Use this book as the cornerstone of your revision and don't hesitate to write in it – personalise your notes and check your progress by ticking off each section as you revise.

Tick to track your progress

Use the revision planner on pages 4–5 to plan your revision, topic by topic. Tick each box when you have:

- revised and understood a topic
- tested yourself
- practised the exam questions and gone online to see the answer guidance.

You can also keep track of your revision by ticking off each topic heading in the book. You may find it helpful to add your own notes as you work through each topic.

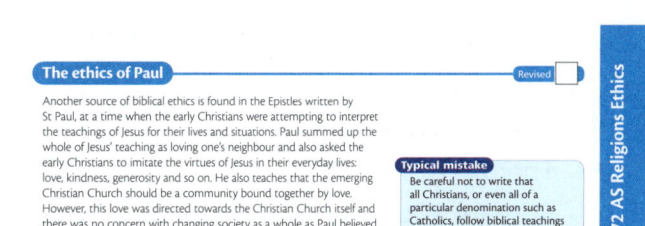

Features to help you succeed

Exam tips

Throughout the book there are tips to help you boost your final grade.

Typical mistakes

Identifies the typical mistakes candidates make and explains how you can avoid them.

Now test yourself

These short, knowledge-based questions provide the first step in testing your learning. Answers are provided at the back of the book

Key words

Clear, concise definitions of essential key terms are provided on the page where they first appear.

Exam practice

Practice exam questions are provided for each chapter. Use them to consolidate your revision and practise your exam skills.

Online

Go online to see the answer guidance to the exam questions at **www.therevisionbutton.co.uk/ myrevisionnotes**.

My revision planner

Exam practice answer guidance at **www.therevisionbutton.co.uk/myrevisionnotes**

Introduction

What is the study of religious ethics about?

The study of religious ethics is the philosophical study of good and bad, what makes something right and what makes something else wrong. It requires you to examine moral issues, such as abortion and euthanasia, and to examine many different ethical approaches to these issues, both religious and secular.

Within the curriculum the focus of citizenship education relates to strands of societal involvement. The AS level Religious Ethics is part of the Religious Studies specification and aims to:

- develop your interest in and enthusiasm for a rigorous study of religious ethics and relate it to the wider world;
- treat the subject as an academic discipline by developing knowledge, understanding and skills appropriate to the specialist study of religious ethics;
- adopt an enquiring, critical and reflective approach to the study of religious ethics;
- reflect on and develop your own values, opinions and attitudes in the light of your learning.

Why study Religious Ethics?

For those who have already studied the OCR Religious Studies B at GCSE, taking AS level Religious Ethics is a natural progression. There is a clear pathway from the work that students do in OCR GCSE Religious Studies and what they have to do in this specification. However, the specifications build on, but do not depend on, the knowledge, understanding and skills specified for GCSE Religious Studies.

What is covered in AS level Religious Studies?

AS level Religious Studies is made up of two units. You can do any combination you like of the following units:

Unit G571: AS Philosophy of Religion

- Ancient Greek influences on philosophy of religion
- Judaeo-Christian influences on philosophy of religion
- Traditional arguments for the existence of God
- Challenges to religious belief

Unit G572: AS Religious Ethics

- Ethical theories
- Applied ethics

Unit G573: AS Jewish Scriptures

- Time line of scriptures
- Form criticism
- Topics

Unit G574: AS New Testament

- First century Gospel setting
- Themes and texts of Mark's passion narrative
- The resurrection in the Synoptic Gospels

Unit G575: AS Developments in Christian Theology

- Foundations of Christian theology
- Liberation theology

Unit G576: AS Buddhism

- Origins of Buddhism
- Core concepts
- Key teachings, attitudes and practices

Unit G577: AS Hinduism

- Origins of Hinduism
- Core concepts
- Key teachings, attitudes and practices

Unit G578: AS Islam

- Background and origins of Islam
- Beliefs
- Practices

G579: AS Judaism

- Sacred writings
- Beliefs
- Practices

Most students study units G571 and G572. This book covers G572: Religious Ethics.

The units are split up into two key areas: ethical theories and applied ethics. In this book, each chapter covers either an ethical theory or an applied ethical issue.

The ethical theories covered are:

- Natural Law
- Kantian ethics
- Utilitarianism
- Religious ethics.

This book only uses Christian ethics as that is what most candidates use. But candidates are free to use the ethics of any of the other religions studied: Buddhism, Judaism, Islam or Hinduism.

The ethical issues covered are:

- abortion
- right to a child
- euthanasia
- war and peace
- foetal research and genetic engineering.

Ethical theories/issues	Ch	Page
Moral Absolutism and Moral Relativism	1	9
Natural Moral Law	2	13
Kantian ethics	3	17
Utilitarianism	4	21
Religious (Christian) ethics	5	26
Abortion	6	31
Right to a child	7	37
Euthanasia	8	40
Genetic engineering and foetal research	9	44
War and peace	10	48

How does the assessment work?

Each exam lasts 1 hour 30 minutes and you are expected to answer two questions from four. Each question is split into two parts, A and B. A relates to (AO1) and B relates to evaluation (AO2).

AO1 focuses on knowledge and understanding – this includes selecting relevant course material to answer the questions set, using examples to demonstrate how the theories work, using subject specific terms and names fluidly in your answers, as well as constructing your essay in a mature and sophisticated manner. This is worth 70 per cent, 25 out of 35 marks.

AO2 focuses on evaluation – you can assess the strengths and weaknesses of a theory by looking at whether it is internally coherent and not hypocritical, or by applying it to fictional situations to see if the conclusions are perverse. You are expected to be able to draw on the criticisms made by other contemporary scholars. This is worth 30 per cent, 10 out of 35 marks.

Assessment Objectives (AO)

Level	Mark/25	AO1	Mark/10	AO2
1	1–5	almost completely ignores the question little relevant material some concepts inaccurate shows little knowledge of technical terms	1–2	very little argument or justification of viewpoint little or no successful analysis views asserted with no justification
Communication: often unclear or disorganised; can be difficult to understand; spelling, punctuation and grammar may be inadequate.				
2	6–10	a basic attempt to address the question knowledge limited and partially accurate limited understanding might address the general topic rather than the question directly selection often inappropriate limited use of technical terms	3–4	a basic attempt to sustain an argument and justify a viewpoint some analysis, but not successful views asserted but little justification
Communication: some clarity and organisation; easy to follow in parts; spelling, punctuation and grammar may be inadequate.				
3	11–15	satisfactory attempt to address the question some accurate knowledge appropriate understanding some successful selection of material some accurate use of technical terms	5–6	the argument is sustained and justified some successful analysis which may be implicit views asserted but not fully justified
Communication: some clarity and organisation; easy to follow in parts; spelling, punctuation and grammar may be inadequate.				
4	16–20	a good attempt to address the question accurate knowledge good understanding good selection of material technical terms mostly accurate	7–8	a good attempt to sustain an argument some successful and clear analysis some effective use of evidence views analysed and developed
Communication: generally clear and organised; can be understood as a whole; spelling, punctuation and grammar good.				
5	21–25	a very good/excellent attempt to address the question showing understanding and engagement with the material very high level of ability to select and deploy relevant information accurate use of technical terms	9–10	a very good/excellent attempt to sustain an argument comprehends the demands of the question uses a range of evidence shows understanding and critical analysis of different viewpoints
Communication: answer is well constructed and organised; easily understood; spelling, punctuation and grammar very good.				

Examples of the full range of question types appear in this guide in the Exam Practice questions.

Countdown to my exams

6–8 weeks to go

- Start by looking at the specification available from **www.ocr.org.uk**. Make sure you know exactly what material you need to revise and the style of the examination. Use the revision planner on pages 4 and 5 to familiarise yourself with the topics.
- Organise your notes, making sure you have covered everything on the specification. The revision planner will help you group your notes into topics.
- Work out a realistic revision plan that will allow you time for relaxation. Set aside days and times for all the subjects that you need to study, and stick to your timetable.
- Set yourself sensible targets. Break your revision down into focused sessions of around 40 minutes, divided by breaks. This books organises the basic facts into short, memorable sections to make revising easier.

Revised ☐

4–6 weeks to go

- Read through the relevant sections of this book and refer to the Exam tips, Typical mistakes and key terms. Tick off the topics as you feel confident about them. Highlight those topics you find difficult and look at them again in detail.
- Test your understanding of each topic by working through the Now test yourself questions in the book. Look up the answers on pages 53–54.
- Make a note of any problem areas as you revise, and ask your teacher to go over these in class.
- Look at past papers. They are one of the best ways to revise and practise your exam skills. Write or prepare planned answers to the exam practice questions provided in this book. See the answer guidance at **www.therevisionbutton.co.uk/myrevisionnotes**.
- Try different revision methods. For example, you can make notes using mind maps, spider diagrams or flash cards.
- Track your progress using the revision planner and give yourself a reward when you have achieved your target.

Revised ☐

One week to go

- Try to fit in at least one more timed practice of an entire past paper and seek feedback from your teacher, comparing your work closely with the mark scheme.
- Check out the revision planner to make sure you haven't missed out any topics. Brush up on any areas of difficulty by talking them over with a friend or getting help from your teacher.
- Attend any revision classes put on by your teacher. Remember, he or she is an expert at preparing people for examinations.

Revised ☐

The day before the examination

- Flick through these Revision Notes for useful reminders, for example the Exam tips, Typical mistakes and key terms.
- Check the time and place of your examination.
- Make sure you have everything you need – extra pens and pencils, tissues, a watch, bottled water, sweets.
- Allow some time to relax and have an early night to ensure you are fresh and alert for the examination.

Revised ☐

My exam

AS Religious Studies: Religious Ethics – G572

Date: ....

Time: ....

Location: ....

1 Introduction to ethical theories

One of the main divisions in ethical theories is between absolute and relativist theories.

Moral absolutism
Revised

Some moral absolute theories have their origins in religion, but not all do. For example, Kant sees duty as the reason for moral actions. Moral absolutism says that moral commands are true for all times, all societies and all people.

Moral absolutists claim that certain things (such as murder) are **objectively** right or wrong and cannot change according to culture. Actions such as murder are intrinsically wrong so they are wrong in themselves. This approach to ethics is simple and easy to apply as an action is always right or wrong regardless of circumstances and it is **deontological** as the consequences are not considered either. The sources of these absolute laws are different according to belief:

- For a theist the source is God.
- For an atheist or agnostic the source might be nature – this might be linked to Plato's Theory of the Forms as there are some things we just seem to know are wrong without being taught.

> **Objectively** means that if something is right or wrong, it is right or wrong irrespective of one's individual or cultural viewpoint – it is absolutely right or wrong.
>
> **Deontological** comes from the Greek word 'deon' meaning duty. When applied to ethics, deontological means that actions are right or wrong in themselves, regardless of the consequences. For example, it is wrong to torture captured soldiers even if you think you would get a good outcome, such as vital information that might end the war more quickly.

Now test yourself
Tested

1 For a theist, who is the source of absolute morality?
2 What does it mean to say something is intrinsically wrong?

Answers on page 53

Religious absolutism – Divine Command Theory
Revised

Many religions have moral absolutist positions where the law is set by the deity or deities. One such example is the Ten Commandments. For many Christians the Bible is believed to be the word of God. Divine Command Theory came from this understanding: something is good because God commands it and wrong because he forbids it. From this point of view morals come from God and God would not command anyone to do bad things as he is **omnibenevolent**. However, there are problems with this view, as God commands Abraham to kill Isaac and Joshua to kill everyone in Jericho. So does this make God immoral or does God have nothing to do with morality?

> **Omnibenevolent** is a term applied to the God of classical theism, meaning that God is all-good.

Plato addressed this question in the Euthyphro Dilemma when Socrates says '... is what is pious loved by the gods, or is it pious because it is loved?' In other words is something good because God says so or does God say it is good because it is good? If something is good because God commands it this could be arbitrary – actions are good or bad according to what God commands at any given moment and if this is the case why bother to worship him? If we do good actions out of obedience to God, are we doing them for the right reasons? Or are we simply doing them out of fear?

Alternatively morality and goodness are separate from God so there is no religious reason to be good and God is no longer seen as all-powerful as goodness is higher than God.

A way out of this dilemma is to consider that God-given free-will requires us to work out for ourselves the right action, or perhaps the rightness or wrongness of an action comes from the fact that actions are right or wrong in themselves and that just as we are created separate from God so are moral laws.

Now test yourself

Tested ☐

3 Explain the problem with saying that something is good because God commands it.

4 Explain the problem with saying God commands something because it is good.

Answers on page 53

Evaluation of absolutism

Revised ☐

- Morality is universal and does not depend on any individual or group.
- Different societies share common values, such as do not murder.
- It allows criticism of the actions or values of different societies. For example, it is possible to condemn actions such as the Holocaust.
- It is possible to make quick ethical decisions.
- It does not account for differences in cultures, situations or different times.
- It can seem harsh and judgemental.

Moral relativism

Revised ☐

Moral relativists say there are no universal objective moral values as these are relative to different societies and different people. Normative relativists reject the idea of absolutism, though in fact there are no ethical theories that are completely relativist: Utilitarianism sees the greatest good for the greatest number as an absolute but it is relative in the way it applies this to an ethical dilemma.

Typical mistake

A common mistake is to say that ethical theories can be neatly divided into absolute and relative – even a relativist will hold one absolute principle: it is wrong to impose absolute moral rules.

Cultural relativism

Revised

This approach says that moral laws differ from society to society as each society develops. As there is much **diversity** across and between cultures there can be no one morality that fits all. This is a common-sense approach as we can also see that moral values change with time. For example, we no longer permit slavery. In this view morality **depends** on the changes within a culture and is right for the culture to which it applies.

Diversity thesis – morality varies as there is such diversity across and within cultures.

Dependency thesis – morality depends on the nature of each individual culture.

Now test yourself
Tested

5   What is cultural relativism?

Answer on page 53

Exam tip

When explaining cultural relativism give clear examples of different ethical actions.

Evaluating relativism

Revised

- Moral relativism is tolerant and respectful of different societies.
- Moral relativism does not assert that the morals of one person or culture are superior to those of another.
- It allows people to make their own moral decisions.
- It does not allow for universal moral laws, such as murder being wrong.
- Moral relativism does not allow the condemnation of evil actions such as genocide.

Now test yourself
Tested

6   List the strengths and weaknesses of absolutism and relativism and then check back to see how many you got right.

Answer on page 53

Deontological and teleological ethics

Revised

Ethical theories can be divided into those which are deontological and those which are **teleological**.

When making ethical decisions, deontological approaches would ask if the action (for example, abortion) is right or wrong. This is an **absolute** approach, so abortion, for example, would be wrong for everyone, everywhere. Intentions are important to deontological approaches as the motives have to be pure and not influenced by self-interest; something which in practice is very hard to achieve so deontological approaches are often rule-based to make the ethical decision clear-cut.

Teleological comes from the Greek word '*telos*' which means end or purpose. Teleological ethics look at the consequences or result of an action to determine whether it is right or wrong.

Absolute means universal and applying to everyone no matter what the situation.

A teleological approach to making ethical decisions, such as abortion, would look at the outcomes (for example, not having a child with a life-threatening disability who would have a short and painful life) and also the purpose (for example, less suffering for both the child and the parents). A good example of a teleological approach to ethics is Utilitarianism (see Chapter 4).

In reality most people make ethical decisions using a mixture of deontological (What ought I to do? What is my duty?) and teleological approaches (How will this affect me? How will this affect other people?).

Exam tip

Some ethical theories have elements of both deontology and teleology, such as Natural Law (see Chapter 2).

Typical mistake

Be careful, if you also do the Philosophy of Religion unit (G571), not to confuse teleological ethical theories with the teleological proofs for the existence of God.

Exam practice

1 **(a)** Explain the concept of relativist morality.   [25]

   (b) 'Relativist ethics are unfair.' Discuss.   [10]

2 **(a)** Explain what is meant by moral absolutism.   [25]

   (b) 'Moral absolutism cannot be justified.' Discuss.   [10]

3 **(a)** Explain the differences between absolute and relative morality.   [25]

   (b) 'Relativist theories give no convincing reason why people should be good.' Discuss.   [10]

4 **(a)** Explain how a moral relativist might approach the issues raised by abortion.   [25]

   (b) 'A relativist approach to the issues raised by abortion leads to wrong moral choices.' Discuss.   [10]

5 **(a)** Explain the differences between deontological and teleological approaches to ethical decision-making.   [25]

   (b) 'The ends justify the means.' Discuss.   [10]

Answer guidance online

Online

Summary

✔ Absolutists say there are universal moral truths.

✔ Absolutists say that moral actions are right or wrong in themselves, regardless of circumstances, culture or opinion.

✔ Absolutists believe that morals are objective.

✔ Deontological ethics are concerned with the action not the consequences.

✔ Relativists say that moral truths vary and they are not universal.

✔ Relativists believe that morals are subjective.

✔ Teleological ethics are concerned with achieving good consequences.

2 Natural Moral Law

The origins of Natural Law Revised

Natural Moral Law is a deontological theory which is based on Aristotle's teleological philosophy. Aristotle thought that everything had a purpose revealed in its natural form or design, and that fulfilling the telos is the supreme 'good' to be sought. For example a 'good' pen is one which fulfils its purpose: it writes. Thomas Aquinas built on this idea and thought that by using our reason we could know our purpose or telos and then we could work out how to achieve it.

> ### Typical mistake
> Many students write that Natural Law is only a religious ethic but this is incorrect. Atheists can also follow Natural Law if they replace God with nature.

> ### Now test yourself
> Tested
>
> 1   On whose ideas did Thomas Aquinas base his theory of Natural Law?
>
> **Answer on page 53**

The use of reason Revised

Aquinas did not argue that morality could be based on reason alone but that human reason given by God was the starting point for morality, and revelation from the Bible and Church teachings adds to this. He believed that as God is good the world he created is also good and exists to reveal God's goodness. This was God's ultimate purpose in creating the world. Human reason is needed to understand and follow the sense of purpose that God, as creator, has given the world. By fulfilling our purpose we become perfect.

Aquinas like Aristotle thought that eudaimonia (human and societal flourishing) is the natural purpose of humans and creation and this can only be achieved by pursuing certain goods, but Aquinas took this a step further and believed that true eudaimonia is union with God. Aquinas assumed the **Synderesis Rule** – that we naturally do good and avoid evil, but that being human we sometimes get things wrong and follow apparent goods (something we think is good but which does not conform to Natural Law and so does not help us achieve eudaimonia). We need to use our reason correctly in order to work out what is a real good (one that conforms to Natural Law) and this means that both the interior act (motive) and the exterior act (the action) need to be correct.

> ### Typical mistakes
> Some students write that Natural Law is about 'doing what comes naturally' which isn't correct – it is based on nature interpreted by human reason.
>
> Also remember that Natural Law is not totally deontological – it does not give you a rigid law that must always be obeyed as it is not always straightforward and there is some flexibility in its application.

> The **Synderesis Rule** is that we know the basic principles of morality and always intend to do good and avoid evil.

> ### Now test yourself
> Tested
>
> 2   What is the Synderesis Rule?
> 3   What is the difference between a real good and an apparent good?
>
> **Answers on page 53**

Primary and secondary precepts

Aquinas saw the **primary precepts** as the way of achieving human purpose. They apply to everyone and are a direct reflection of divine law in the Bible.

The primary precepts are:

- the preservation of life
- reproduction
- education and learning
- living peacefully in society
- worshipping God.

The primary precepts are descriptive and tell us what human reason says is right and the **secondary precepts** help to put this into practice and tell us what ought to be.

In order to apply the secondary precepts it is necessary to use reason and to understand that these may change as society changes and our knowledge increases, or as the situation demands it. The secondary precepts make the understanding of Natural Law more flexible.

The diagram below shows how Natural Law might work in practice:

> The **primary precepts** are the fundamental principles of Natural Law.
>
> The **secondary precepts** are worked out from the primary precepts of Natural Law and are more flexible.

Exam tip

This movement from an 'is' to an 'ought' is a form of the Naturalistic Fallacy (David Hume). Facts do not need to lead to values. For example, the fact that sex leads to reproduction does not mean that every sexual act must be for reproduction.

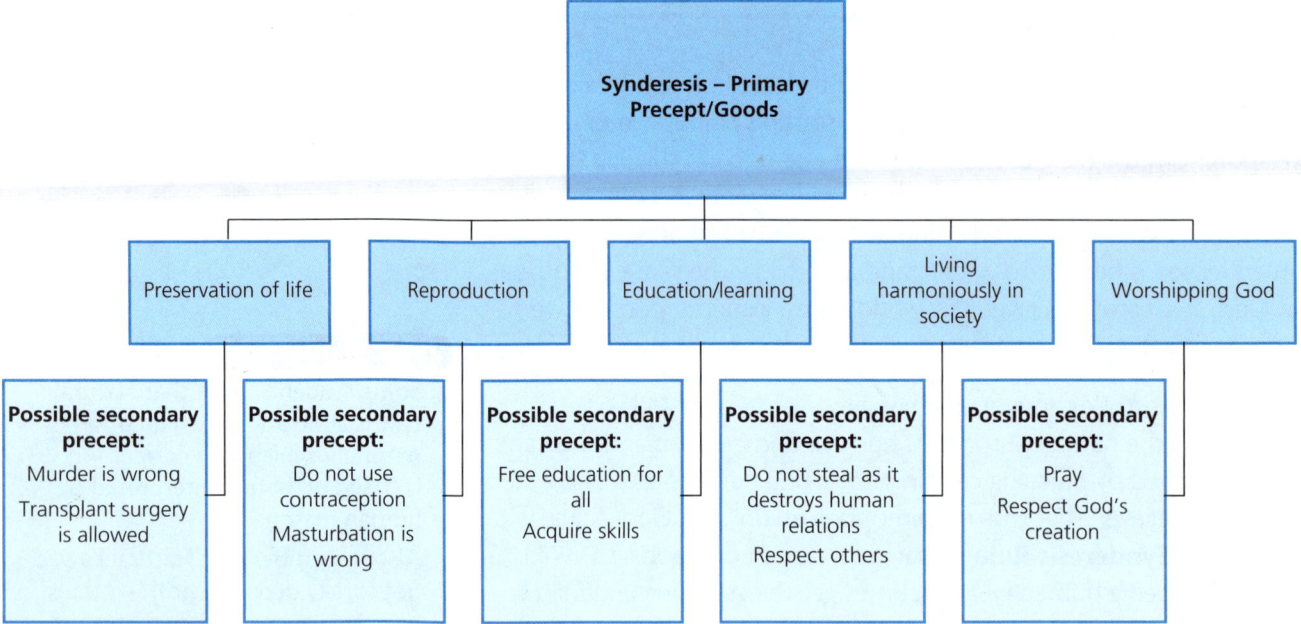

Synderesis – Primary Precept/Goods

Preservation of life	Reproduction	Education/learning	Living harmoniously in society	Worshipping God
Possible secondary precept: Murder is wrong. Transplant surgery is allowed	**Possible secondary precept:** Do not use contraception. Masturbation is wrong	**Possible secondary precept:** Free education for all. Acquire skills	**Possible secondary precept:** Do not steal as it destroys human relations. Respect others	**Possible secondary precept:** Pray. Respect God's creation

Now test yourself
Tested

4 Explain the importance of the primary precepts.
5 List the five primary precepts.

Answers on page 53

The doctrine of double effect
Revised

Aquinas said that the primary precepts are true for everyone – they are absolute. But sometimes we cannot do good without a bad consequence. The **doctrine of double effect** explains that this bad consequence must not be intended. Even though it may be foreseen, it must be an unintended side-effect. The killing of civilians in war is an example of double effect.

> The **doctrine of double effect** is an action where the intention is good but may have bad side-effects. The good intention makes the action good.

Evaluation of Natural Law
Revised

- It is a simple and clear-cut approach to morality.
- The basic principles of preserving human life, reproduction and so on, are common to all societies.
- It allows humans to use reason to work out how to live.
- The secondary precepts allow a degree of flexibility.
- It sees human nature as simple and fixed (heterosexual) but evidence shows that this is not the case.
- Natural Law can be criticised using the Naturalistic Fallacy.
- It has an optimistic view of human nature which does not seem to take account of the Fall.
- It can be interpreted too rigidly and so cannot cope with individual moral problems.

Typical mistake

When evaluating Natural Law students often just discuss the rigidness, inflexibility and the 'old-fashioned' approach of it. It's important to also consider the flexibility in the secondary precepts and that in Natural Law there is a place for practical wisdom in applying the secondary precepts.

Exam practice

1 **(a)** Explain Natural Law theory. **[25]**

   (b) 'Natural Law is not the best approach to euthanasia.' Discuss. **[10]**

2 **(a)** Explain how a follower of Natural Law might respond to issues raised by genetic engineering. **[25]**

   (b) 'All genetic engineering is ethically justified.' Discuss. **[10]**

3 **(a)** Explain how a follower of Natural Law might approach the issues surrounding abortion. **[25]**

   (b) 'Natural law has no serious weaknesses.' Discuss. **[10]**

4 **(a)** Explain how Natural Law theory can be used to decide the right moral action. **[25]**

   (b) To what extent is Natural Law the best approach to ethical decision-making? **[10]**

Answer guidance online

Online

Summary

- Natural Law is a deontological theory, based on a teleological world view.
- Natural Law is living in accordance with our true nature.
- Our purpose as humans can be discovered using our God-given reason.
- The primary precepts enable humans to achieve their true purpose.
- The secondary precepts are derived from the primary precepts and are more flexible.
- Humans sometimes do bad things because they are pursuing apparent goods.
- Both the intention and the act are important.

3 Kantian ethics

Kantian ethics are deontological (right or wrong in itself and about duty) and absolute (universal and applying to everyone no matter what the situation).

Now test yourself

Tested ☐

1   What does deontological mean?

Answer on page 53

Duty and good will

Revised ☐

Kant said that we have an innate moral **duty** revealed through our reason; this he referred to as 'the moral law within'. He said that to act morally is to do one's duty and we should do it for no other reason than it is our duty – it is right.

Kant argued that the highest form of good is **good will** and to have good will is to do one's duty. We should act out of duty not emotion, or self-interest or even compassion. These are good but our actions should be based on reason.

Kant said it was not our duty to do something that is impossible for us to do. For Kant if we ought to do something then it is logically possible for us to do it – 'ought' implies 'can'. This makes moral statements prescriptive – the statement 'I ought to do X' implies 'I can do X'.

> **Duty** – for Kant doing good means rationally determining and doing your duty. Duty is your motive for acting in a moral way.
>
> **Good will** – making a moral choice expresses a good will. It is the resolve to act in such a way that we fulfil our duty.

Now test yourself

Tested ☐

2   What does Kant mean by good will?
3   Why is duty important to Kant?

Answers on page 53

Moral statements

Revised ☐

Kant believed there were two types of statement:

1   *A priori* analytic, for example 1+1=2 – this statement is true in itself.
2   *A posteriori* synthetic, for example, 'It is sunny today' – this statement can be tested and can be true or false.

Kant said that moral statements were *a priori* synthetic. We cannot prove what someone should do just by seeing, so moral statements are *a priori*. But moral statements may or may not be true so they are synthetic.

> **Typical mistake**
>
> Students often use phrases like *a priori* but don't know what they mean! If you cannot remember what they mean it's better to leave them out.

The Categorical Imperative

According to Kant, moral statements can only be known through reason, because they are *a priori* and so there must be a method to work out if a statement is true or false. This method he called the **Categorical Imperative**.

The Categorical Imperative helps us know what our duty is. It applies universally. It is a framework to help us discover which moral statements are true and which are false. Kant contrasts it with the **Hypothetical Imperative** which is conditional 'If I want X then I ought to do Y'. The Hypothetical Imperative is *not* moral.

> **Categorical Imperative** means a command to perform actions that are absolute moral rules that do not consider consequences.
>
> **Hypothetical Imperative** means an action that achieves some goal or end.

> **Exam tip**
>
> When explaining the Hypothetical and Categorical Imperatives use examples. Good responses often use Kant's own examples.

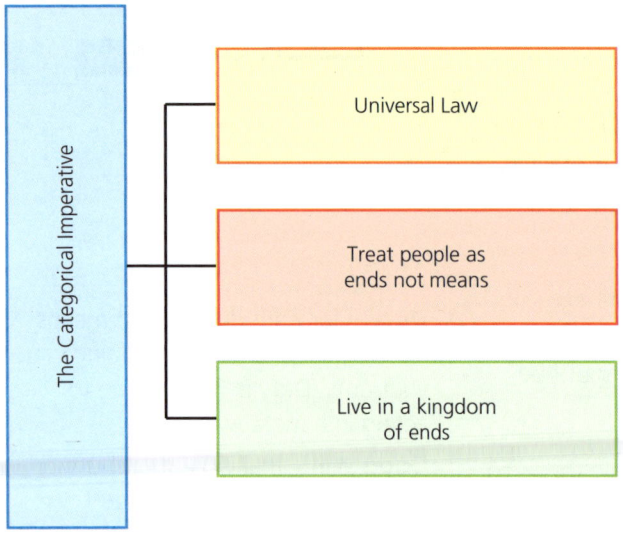

There are three main categorical imperatives:

1 Universal Law – all moral statements should be general laws which apply to everyone in all circumstances without exception. Exceptions will be a contradiction in nature. For example, Kant suggests that promise-keeping should be universalised because a world where everyone failed to keep promises means that promise-keeping would no longer exist. This is known as the **universalisation** of **maxims**.

2 Treat humans as ends in themselves – people should be treated as autonomous and rational. People are worthy of respect and should not be used as a means to get something else. This promotes equality.

3 Act as if you live in a **kingdom of ends** – Kant assumed that a community of all rational people could deduce whether an argument was moral or not through their reason and so all should have the same moral laws. Kantian ethics are social and democratic.

> **Universalisation** means a moral law which is obeyed at all times everywhere.
>
> **Maxims** are general rules or laws.
>
> **Kingdom of ends** – in Kantian ethics this means a world in which people do not treat others as means but only as ends.

Now test yourself

Tested ☐

4   What is the Hypothetical Imperative?
5   List the three formulations of the Categorical Imperative.

Answers on page 53

Freedom

Revised ☐

Kant believes we are free to make rational choices. Reason is what distinguishes us from animals. We have to be free to do our duty. If we cannot be free we cannot be moral agents and 'ought' no longer implies 'can'.

Summmum bonum

Revised ☐

The **summum bonum** or 'supreme good' is virtue plus happiness. We should not act in order to get happiness, but the virtuous person has good will. Happiness in this life is not certain and bad things happen to good people, so the summum bonum is achieved in the afterlife. For Kant, morality leads to God and God is necessary for morality.

> **Summum bonum** means the supreme good that we pursue through moral actions.

Evaluation of Kantian ethics

Revised ☐

- The Categorical Imperative forbids acts that most people think are wrong, such as theft.
- The Categorical Imperative protects the dignity and equality of everyone. Everyone is treated fairly.
- Universalisability is difficult in today's world as not everyone has the same moral views.
- Conflicting duties are a problem – do you tell a lie or save a life?
- Kant does not consider consequences and most people think they do matter.
- It is inflexible as it is an absolute theory which applies in all situations.

> **Typical mistake**
>
> When evaluating Kant don't forget to discuss conflicting duties and to give examples.

> **Exam tip**
>
> You will see in the exam practice section below, how sometimes applied ethics questions are in part (a) and sometimes in part (b). Be careful in part (a) to explain just Kant's approach to the issue; do not try to evaluate as it will not count towards your answer. When discussing issues in part (b) you must give a balanced response. Sometimes the issues are controversial, but you must give both sides of the argument. As well as adopting and justifying a particular viewpoint you need to counter opposing arguments.

Exam practice

1 **(a)** Explain Kant's theory of duty. [25]

  (b) To what extent is Kant's theory a good approach to embryo research? [10]

2 **(a)** Explain, with examples, Kant's theory of duty. [25]

  (b) 'Kant's ethical theory has no serious weaknesses.' Discuss. [10]

3 **(a)** Explain Kant's argument for using the Categorical Imperative. [25]

  (b) 'The universalisation of maxims by Kant cannot be defended.' Discuss. [10]

4 **(a)** Explain how a follower of Kantian ethics might approach issues surrounding the right to a child. [25]

  (b) 'The right to a child is an absolute right.' Discuss. [10]

5 **(a)** Explain Kant's ethical theory. [25]

  (b) 'Kant's theory of ethics is not a useful approach to abortion.' Discuss. [10]

Answer guidance online

Online

Summary

- ✔ Deontological ethics are concerned with actions not consequences.
- ✔ Kant's theory is deontological because it is based on duty. To act morally is to do one's duty and obey the moral law.
- ✔ 'Ought' implies 'can'.
- ✔ Moral statements are *a priori synthetic* (reason, not sense experience and can be proved true or false).
- ✔ We should act out of duty, not emotion.

- ✔ Moral statements are categorical – they prescribe and the result is not the most important when making an ethical decision.
- ✔ The Hypothetical Imperative is not moral as it depends on the result.
- ✔ The Categorical Imperative shows what your duty is.
- ✔ Humans are free to make rational choices. They need to be free to make moral choices.

Exam practice answer guidance at **www.therevisionbutton.co.uk/myrevisionnotes**

4 Utilitarianism

Utilitarianism is a teleological or consequentialist approach to ethics which argues that something is good or bad according to its benefit for the majority of people. Bentham, who was the first person to formalise this theory in the way we know it today, called this the **principle of Utility**: the greatest good for the greatest number. It is the consequences of an action which judge whether it is good or bad.

> The **principle of Utility** is often known as the greatest happiness principle. It is about the greatest good for the greatest number.

Now test yourself   Tested ☐

1 What is the principle of Utility?

Answer on page 53

Bentham's Utilitarianism   Revised ☐

Bentham did not believe that morality was based on the authority of God but on the authority of nature and specifically on the belief that one moral good equals pleasures and one evil equals pain: happiness equals pleasure minus pain.

In order to put his ideas into practice Bentham devised the **Hedonic Calculus** as a way of measuring pleasure and so calculating the consequences of an action. The seven criteria are:

- **P**urity (meaning that it is not followed by pain)
- **R**emoteness (how near or far the pleasure is)
- **I**ntensity (how deep the pleasure is)
- **C**ertainty (how certain or uncertain the pleasure is)
- **E**xtent (how universal the pleasure is, how many people are affected)
- **D**uration (how long the pleasure will last)
- **F**ecundity (meaning the chance that it will produce more pleasure)

This method is **quantitative** – it measures the quantity of pleasure.

> **Hedonic Calculus** – Bentham's way of measuring the good and bad effects of an action.
>
> **Quantitative** means something that can be measured. The Hedonic Calculus is quantitative, that is it measures how much pleasure is gained from an action.

Now test yourself   Tested ☐

2 Is Bentham's version of Utilitarianism best described as quantitative or qualitative?
3 List the seven elements of the Hedonic Calculus.

Answers on page 53

Exam tip

There is not a lot to write about Bentham's Utilitarianism so make sure that you know and can explain the Hedonic Calculus and are able to apply it to ethical issues such as abortion.

Evaluation of Bentham's Utilitarianism

Revised

- It sees all pleasures as of equal value and promotes the well-being of the majority.
- It leaves the minority at the mercy of the majority – Bentham rejects human rights.
- It needs both knowledge and time to make a decision using the Hedonic Calculus.
- It is difficult to predict consequences.
- There is potential to justify evil acts if this makes the majority happy – there is no notion of absolute right and wrong.
- It is common sense to think of consequences when making an ethical decision.
- It is straightforward and based on a single principle.

Mill's Utilitarianism

Revised

John Stuart Mill did not agree with the following aspects of Bentham's Utilitarianism:

- giving equal value to all pleasures (he said it was 'swine philosophy')
- the emphasis on pleasure alone
- the treatment of minorities.

Mill stressed the idea of happiness (along the lines of Aristotle's Virtue Ethics) rather than pleasure as it was motivated more by sympathy for others and **autonomy** (the free choice of the individual). He also modified the principle of Utility to a **qualitative** approach – looking at higher pleasures as being of greater quality than lower pleasures '… better to be Socrates dissatisfied than a pig satisfied'. Higher pleasures, such as music and reading, he saw as of greater value than lower pleasures, such as food, drink and football. Higher pleasures are those of the mind and lower ones of the body. He thought that higher pleasures led to human progress.

Mill also thought that making the minority accept the wishes of the majority would not make for a good society. He thought that what is good for one person is good for all. He called this the principle of universalisability, and this meant that human rights were important as was the **Golden Rule** of Jesus: 'Do unto others as you would have them do unto you.'

> **Autonomy** means self-rule: someone who makes moral decisions freely is said to be an autonomous moral agent.
>
> **Qualitative** means the quality of something rather than the amount of it. Mill looks at the quality of the pleasure not how much pleasure there is.

> **Typical mistake**
>
> Students often confuse Mill's idea of happiness with Bentham's idea of pleasure but it is actually closer to Aristotle's idea of personal and societal flourishing.

> **Now test yourself**
>
> Tested
>
> 4 What are Mill's objections to Bentham's Utilitarianism?
> 5 Is Mill's version of Utilitarianism best described as quantitative or qualitative?
>
> **Answers on page 53**

> The **Golden Rule** is the teaching of Jesus that we should treat others as we would like to be treated.

Evaluation of Mill's Utilitarianism

Revised

- It is difficult to predict consequences.
- It is difficult to tell the differences between higher and lower pleasures or even between higher pleasures.
- The whole idea of higher pleasures can seem a bit snobbish.
- Progress is not necessarily only made by higher pleasures.
- It attempts to give equal rights to all.
- It is still difficult to protect the minorities.

Comparing Bentham and Mill

Revised

Jeremy Bentham	John Stuart Mill
The greatest good (pleasure) for the greatest number	The greatest happiness for the greatest number
Aims at the individual	Aims for the good of all
Quantitative – Hedonic Calculus	Qualitative
All pleasures are of the same value	Higher and lower pleasures
No consideration of human rights	Individual liberty is vital
Consequentialist	Consequentialist

Act and Rule Utilitarianism

Revised

Act Utilitarianism is often linked to Bentham's approach. It follows the one rule – the greatest good for the greatest number. So an action is only right if it promotes happiness. Laws are rules of thumb that can be disregarded if the circumstances require it.

Rule Utilitarianism argues that moral rules, based on the principle of Utility and for the benefit of society should be kept by everyone in similar circumstances. These rules benefit everyone and stop the principle of Utility being used for subjective purposes.

- Strong Rule Utilitarians believe the rule should always be kept.
- Weak Rule Utilitarians believe the rule can be broken in situations where better consequences might be achieved by breaking the rule and taking an Act Utilitarian approach.

Mill is often linked to Rule Utilitarianism though he never gave himself this title and in reality he is more of a Weak Rule Utilitarian.

Typical mistake

Be careful not to say categorically that Mill is a Rule Utilitarian. You could say he was the originator of Rule Utilitarianism and Bentham the originator of Act Utilitarianism.

Peter Singer's Preference Utilitarianism

Revised

Preference Utilitarianism is based on the idea that a good action is one that maximises the preferences of all involved so that my own wants, needs and desires cannot count for more than those of anyone else. Happiness is maximised by allowing people to satisfy as many of their first preferences as possible. This means that the preferences and interests of all those involved must be considered, which means that love and relationships do not count. To make an ethical decision it is necessary to take an impartial view: that of the **impartial spectator**.

An **impartial spectator** is someone who does not count their own preferences as more important than the preferences of others. It is someone who can take an objective rather than a subjective view.

Singer says society is made up of a collection of individuals, each with their own preferences, so trade-offs have to be made for the general welfare of that society – in other words some preferences have to be accepted and others rejected so that the good of all may be achieved.

Peter Singer is often known as the philosopher of the Animal Liberation Movement as he extends his idea of Preference Utilitarianism to all sentient creatures. He approves of Bentham's dictum: 'the question is not, "can they reason?" Nor "can they talk?" But, "can they suffer?"' and agrees with Mill when he suggests extending morality to the whole of sentient creation. Singer accords animals rights as sentient (feeling) beings; they have valid interests. Not to consider them is to be guilty of **speciesism**. So eating meat, consuming battery-farmed eggs, cosmetic testing on animals, or wearing fur are wrong, as according to Singer, animals would prefer these things not to be done.

> **Speciesism** means giving moral preference to the interests of one's own species, over identical interests of members of a different species. Speciesism is an unjustified bias from Singer's perspective (similar to a racist or sexist bias in favour of the well-being of members of one's own race or sex).

Evaluation of Singer's Utilitarianism

Revised

- Preference Utilitarianism tries to broaden out our moral decisions to include their global impact.
- Singer does not consider those who cannot state their preferences such as infants and those with advanced Alzheimer's.
- It is difficult for people to consider a wide range of interests and always put themselves in other's shoes – sometimes family and commitments come first.
- Preferences change over time and this can be difficult to keep up with.

Evaluation of Utilitarianism

Revised

- It is straightforward and aims for a happier life for most people.
- When we act it is normal to consider the consequences.
- It enables people to consider other viewpoints when making an ethical decision.
- It is democratic.
- It is difficult to predict consequences.
- It can lead to actions that would be considered bad as there is no sense of absolute right and wrong.
- It does not protect minorities and so can lead to injustice.
- It does not consider motives or intentions and does not treat people with intrinsic value.
- It is impersonal and does not consider the rights of the individual.

> **Exam tip**
>
> Remember that Utilitarianism is also applied to the ethical issues studied at A2.

Tested

Now test yourself

6   Complete the following diagram and then check back to see how you can improve it.

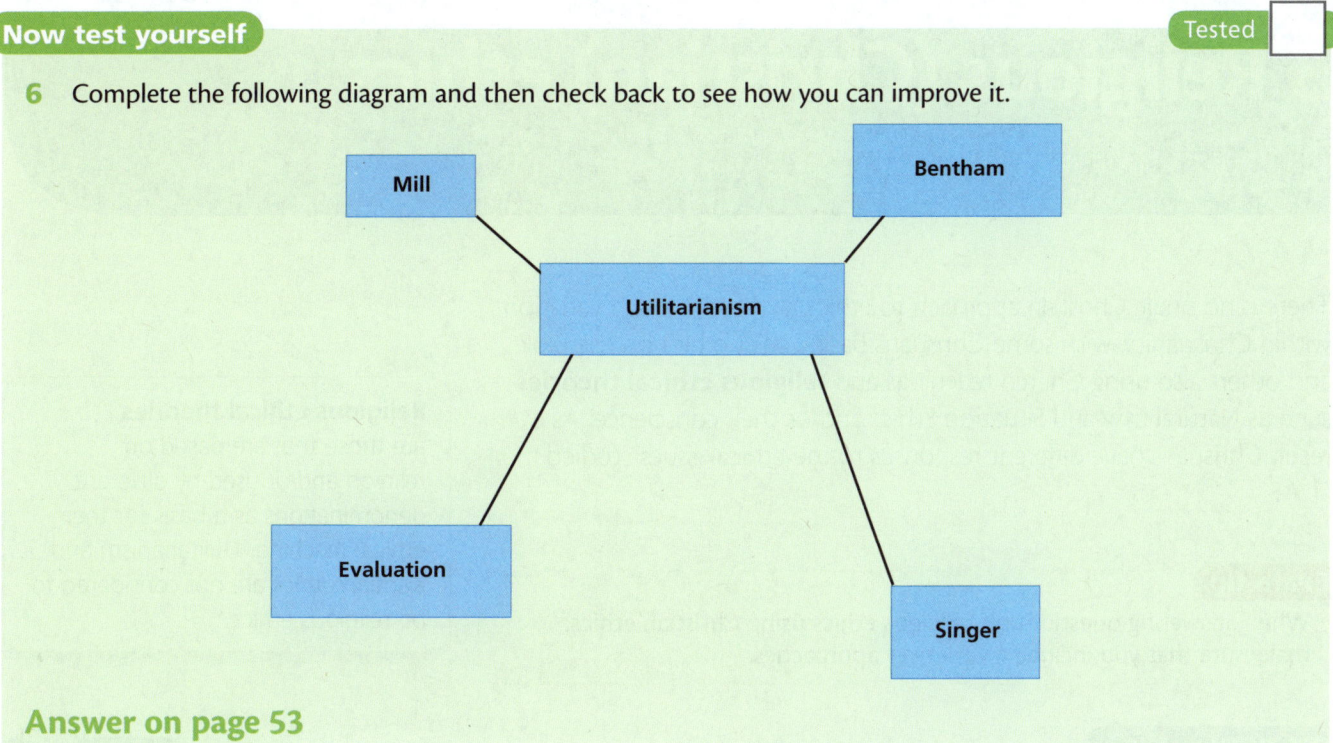

Mill

Bentham

Utilitarianism

Evaluation

Singer

Answer on page 53

Exam practice

1   (a) Explain how Bentham's version of Utilitarianism can be used to decide the right course of action.   [25]

(b) 'Utilitarianism is the best approach to euthanasia.' Discuss.   [10]

2   (a) Explain how Utilitarians approach the issues of war.   [25]

(b) 'Pacifism causes more harm than good.' Discuss.   [10]

3   (a) Explain Mill's version of Utilitarianism.   [25]

(b) 'Utilitarianism can lead to wrong moral decisions.' Discuss.   [10]

4   (a) Explain the main differences between Act and Rule Utilitarianism.   [25]

(b) To what extent is Utilitarianism a useful method of making decisions about euthanasia?   [10]

5   (a) Explain the Preference Utilitarianism of Peter Singer.   [25]

(b) To what extent is Preference Utilitarianism the best form of Utilitarianism?   [10]

Answer guidance online

Online

Summary

✔ Utilitarianism is teleological and depends on consequences to judge if an action is good or bad.

✔ The rightness or wrongness of an action is tested by the principle of Utility – the amount of pleasure or happiness caused by the action.

✔ Bentham's approach is quantitative and uses the Hedonic Calculus to calculate if an action is good or not.

✔ John Stuart Mill considers the well-being of autonomous individuals acting for their own well-being and that of society.

✔ Mill focuses on quality pleasures and divided pleasures into higher (of the mind) and lower (of the body).

✔ Act Utilitarianism says that a good action is one which produces the most pleasure in a particular situation. Act Utilitarianism is flexible as it takes account of different circumstances.

✔ Rule Utilitarians use rules based on the principle of Utility which will give the best result to all concerned.

✔ Preference Utilitarianism is associated with Peter Singer and considers the preferences of all involved equally. It requires people to be impartial spectators and not to consider their own preferences above those of others.

✔ Singer considers the preferences of all sentient beings.

5 Religious (Christian) ethics

There is no single Christian approach to ethics as there is much variation within Christianity, with some Christians basing their ethics on the Bible and others also using Church teachings and **religious ethical theories** such as Natural Law and Situation Ethics and/or their conscience. As a result Christians have different responses to the ethical issues studied at AS.

> **Religious ethical theories** are those that are based on religion and/or used by different denominations as a basis for their ethical teaching. Utilitarianism and Kantian ethics are not considered to be religious ethics.

> **Exam tip**
>
> When answering questions on religious ethics using Christian ethics, make sure that you include a variety of approaches.

Biblical ethics   Revised ☐

Most Christians today do not follow all the laws found in the Bible but many of the moral laws still hold true such as the Ten Commandments. Christian denominations also tend to focus on particular biblical teachings that fit their own beliefs, for example, teachings on divorce or homosexuality.

> **Now test yourself**   Tested ☐
>
> 1 Do all Christians follow the teachings in the Bible exactly?
>
> **Answer on page 53**

The ethics of Jesus   Revised ☐

The ethical teaching of Jesus seems to be summed up in one word: love. This love is central to the relationship with God and with others: 'Love God. … and love your neighbour as yourself.' This became the basis of what is now known as the Golden Rule: 'Do to others as you would have them do to you (Matthew 7:12).

Jesus' Sermon on the Mount (Matthew 5–7) describes this moral teaching and how to put it into practice. Luke's Gospel in particular shows how it can be put into practice through helping the poor and dispossessed.

> **Now test yourself**   Tested ☐
>
> 2 What is the Golden Rule?
>
> **Answer on page 53**

The ethics of Paul

Another source of biblical ethics is found in the Epistles written by St Paul, at a time when the early Christians were attempting to interpret the teachings of Jesus for their lives and situations. Paul summed up the whole of Jesus' teaching as loving one's neighbour and also asked the early Christians to imitate the virtues of Jesus in their everyday lives: love, kindness, generosity and so on. He also teaches that the emerging Christian Church should be a community bound together by love. However, this love was directed towards the Christian Church itself and there was no concern with changing society as a whole as Paul believed that God would soon come and establish his kingdom.

The teaching of love for one's neighbour did eventually lead to Christians taking a lead in social responsibility and was instrumental in the teaching of Situation Ethics in the 1960s.

> **Typical mistake**
>
> Be careful not to write that all Christians, or even all of a particular denomination such as Catholics, follow biblical teachings literally. Catholics also use the magisterium – teachings which come from the Pope and/or the bishops, mostly through encyclicals (letters addressed to all members of the Church). Christians of all denominations also use prayer and their consciences to help them make moral decisions.

> **Now test yourself**
>
> Tested
>
> 3 Why did Paul have very little social teaching compared to Luke's Gospel?
>
> 4 What is the magisterium?
>
> **Answers on page 53**

Divine Command Theory

Divine Command Theory is based on the idea of God's omnipotence and that, as Creator, he orders the universe by his Divine Law which humans should obey. This Divine Law is revealed in the Bible and in the teachings of the Church. God would never command anything contrary to his nature and would only command what is morally good. This is an important issue as it basically asks whether morality and religion are linked or totally separate and what this says about God. Divine Command Theory says that actions are right or wrong depending on whether they follow God's commands or not.

This is an objective and deontological approach and stresses the importance of obedience to and duty to God.

The main problems with Divine Command Theory for Christians is knowing exactly what God's will is and the fact that God has given people **free will** to work out the right ethical decisions for themselves. Additionally, biblical teachings themselves are not always clear and require quite a leap to put into practice. For example, does the biblical teaching that we are made in the image of God mean that abortion is wrong, or does the teaching 'Go forth and multiply' mean that contraception is against the will of God?

> **Free will** is the God-given ability to make free decisions and choices.

Religious ethical theories – Natural Law, Situation Ethics

Natural Law is dealt with in Chapter 2.

Situation Ethics is based on the Christian principle of love and is explained by Joseph Fletcher who argued that we should do the most loving action (**agape** or sacrificial love) in each situation. This agapaeic love is non-negotiable and absolute but in every other way Situation Ethics is relative and teleological (it looks for the best consequences). It is both absolute in its adherence to agape but also relative and teleological in its approach to ethical issues.

Fletcher uses four working principles:

1 Pragmatism – the decision must work in practice.
2 Relativism – there are no fixed rules except agape.
3 Positivism – decisions are based on agape not reason.
4 Personalism – people come before rules and laws.

These four working principles are based on six fundamental principles:

1 Agape is the only absolute good.
2 All decisions should be based on agape.
3 Agape and justice are the same.
4 Agape does not have favourites – everyone is to be treated equally.
5 The end justifies the means.
6 Decisions vary according to the situation.

Situation Ethics takes individuals into account and puts love at the centre of ethical decision-making and it is flexible enough to consider different situations. But agape is very demanding and so can be easily manipulated as there is no objectivity.

> **Typical mistake**
>
> Candidates often interpret Natural Law as a series of fixed laws and obligations, but Aquinas did not see it in this way: he meant that our nature is knowable through our reason and so ethics is concerned with our common humanity not a set of rules by which we make moral decisions. That which is absolutely wrong is anything which is against our true purpose: so some absolutes such as the **Sanctity of Life** will never change whatever the situation.

> **Sanctity of Life** is the teaching that all human life is sacred and special as we are made in God's image. The belief that human life is valuable in itself.
>
> **Agape** is from one of the Greek words meaning love – a love that is different from liking, familial love or erotic love. For Christians it means the unconditional love that must be shown to others.

> **Now test yourself**
>
> Tested
>
> 5 What is Situation Ethics based on?
> 6 What are the four working principles of Situation Ethics?
>
> **Answers on page 53**

Conscience

Revised

Catholics say that conscience plays an important part in ethical decision-making. By conscience, they mean not a feeling or the voice of God but reason and judgement. Conscience can be mistaken so it needs to be educated and formed.

For Quakers conscience is an inner light, which is God guiding them to make the right decisions.

Are religious ethics absolutist or relativist?

Revised

Religion can be a source of moral absolutes, but the command to love one another can lead to more relativistic decisions. Different interpretations of the Bible among liberal and fundamentalist Christians also lead to different approaches.

The challenge of Situation Ethics to traditional Catholic teaching led to the idea of **Proportionalism** – a compromise between Natural Law and Situation Ethics. Proportionalism accepts, like Natural Law, that certain actions are wrong in themselves, but that the wrong action may be the right thing to do if there is a proportionate reason to do it. (This idea can also be found in **Just War theory**.)

Looking at the teaching of Jesus we also find that religious ethics can be both absolute and relative: Jesus upheld the authority of the law but also taught that the law is subject to humanity. For example, he healed on the Sabbath and famously proclaimed that the Sabbath was made for man not man for the Sabbath.

> **Proportionalism** says an action can be right if there is a proportional reason to break an established law. In other words, a proportionalist maintains that there are basic moral laws which can be broken in extreme circumstances.
>
> **Just War theory** is a set of rules about when it is just to go to war, and just ways to fight and end a war. (See Chapter 10.)

Evaluating Christian ethics

Revised

There is a wide variety of approaches to Christian ethical decision-making. For Catholics it involves Natural Law, Church teaching, conscience and **Virtue Ethics**. Other Christian denominations have various ethical approaches, from the very liberal protestant Situation Ethics to the more conservative and absolutist understanding of biblical teaching.

Some Christians will take one approach while others will use a combination. This means it is almost impossible to generalise about Christian approaches to moral issues: conservative Christians might oppose abortion, euthanasia, sex before marriage and homosexuality for example, while other Christians take different views. Quakers will take a **pacifist** view of war, although pacifists are to be found in all Christian denominations. Other Christians will follow the Just War theory. Even within Christian traditions that require their followers to keep moral rules there will be those who disagree and yet remain within that tradition.

> **Virtue Ethics** concerns habitually doing what is right. To be a good person requires practising virtuous behaviour.
>
> **Pacifism** is the belief that acts of violence are always wrong. A follower of pacifism is called a pacifist.

Exam practice

1 **(a)** Explain the ethical teachings of the religion you have studied. [25]

    (b) 'Some religious ethics are too rigid for modern decision-making.' Discuss. [10]

2 **(a)** Explain how the ethics of the religion you have studied might be applied to abortion. [25]

    (b) 'Religious ethics fail to consider consequences.' Discuss. [10]

3 **(a)** Explain the ethical principles of the religion you have studied in relation to war. [25]

    (b) 'War should not be allowed even as a last resort.' Discuss. [10]

4 **(a)** Explain how the followers of the religion you have studied make ethical decisions. [25]

    (b) 'Morality and religion are separate.' Discuss. [10]

5 **(a)** Explain the main ethical principles of the religion you have studied with regard to genetic engineering. [25]

    (b) 'Religious ethics prevents progress in genetic engineering.' Discuss. [10]

6 **(a)** Explain how the followers of the religion you have studied justify going to war. [25]

    (b) 'Religious believers should be pacifist.' Discuss. [10]

Answer guidance online

Online

Summary

- ✔ There is no one Christian ethical teaching.
- ✔ Christians will have different ethical views on ethical issues such as abortion, genetic engineering and so on.
- ✔ Christian ethical teachings come from:
  - The Bible, which can be interpreted in a variety of ways.
- The teachings of the Church and tradition. (Catholics call this the magisterium.)
- Religious normative ethical theories such as Natural law and Situation Ethics.
- The individual's conscience.
- A mixture of all the above.

6 Abortion

Why abortion is an ethical issue

Revised

- People disagree about when life begins.
- People disagree about whether abortion is murder.
- People disagree about whether a woman has the right to choose.
- People argue over the time limit for abortions.
- People disagree over whether the life of an embryo and/or foetus is sacred.
- People disagree over whether to abort a disabled foetus and what constitutes severe disability.

Issues surrounding abortion

Revised

- Does the Sanctity of Life apply to a foetus? Is all life sacred? Whose life is more sacred – that of the mother or that of the unborn child?
- When is the foetus a person? When does life begin? Does a foetus have the qualities of **personhood**?
- What makes a good **Quality of Life**? Who decides? Whose Quality of Life is more important – that of the mother or that of the unborn child?
- Whose rights are more important – the mother's or the foetus'?

> **Personhood** is a definition of a human being as a person: having consciousness, self-awareness, ability to reason and self-sufficiency.
>
> **Quality of Life** means the kind of life a person has or will have. It's related to the belief that human life is not valuable in itself (as the teaching of the Sanctity of Life believes) but is dependent on what kind of life it is and whether it is worth living.

Now test yourself
Tested

1. List the four main ethical issues surrounding abortion.
2. Which of these issues would a follower of Natural Law consider to be the most important?

Answers on page 53

Exam tip
Exam questions usually centre round the issues surrounding abortion, NOT just on abortion, so you need to read the question carefully and address the above issues.

The concept of the Sanctity of Life as applied to abortion

Revised

Christianity emphasises the importance of the Sanctity of Life: 'So God created humankind in his image' (Genesis 1:27). (known as Imago Dei).

The teaching implies that, as God is the creator of life, he alone says when it starts and ends. All life is equal, has intrinsic value, and should be treated with reverence and respect. This is also part of the teaching of Natural Law as taking life is seen as intrinsically evil, and all unborn life should be protected.

Abortion can only be justified using the doctrine of double effect. For example, an ectopic pregnancy may be terminated, as the intention is to preserve the life of the mother not to kill the foetus.

- Strong Sanctity of Life – all life, both born and unborn is to be respected. Abortion is never allowed whatever the circumstances.
- Weak Sanctity of Life – life in general is to be respected but scientific advances mean that the boundaries between life and death are more flexible and we know more about foetal disabilities. Sometimes it is necessary to apply love and compassion and allow abortion whether to avoid a life-time of suffering for the child or to consider the mental and physical health of the mother.

Problems with the Sanctity of Life

- Charles Darwin challenged Imago Dei with his theory of natural selection.
- Kant saw no reason to link vital signs (heart beating, brain waves and so on) to valuing life.
- Peter Singer – speciesism, meaning that all life should be valued not just human life.
- The Sanctity of Life cannot cope with a conflict of duties – which life is more sacred: that of the mother or that of the unborn child?
- Sometimes it means that the life of a foetus is given more value than that of a disabled person, a mentally ill person, a criminal and so on.

The concept of personhood as applied to abortion

Revised

Questions to consider:
- Is the embryo an actual person or a potential person or neither?
- What characteristics make a person?
- If an embryo isn't a person, when does a foetus become a person?
- Does personhood depend on when life begins?
- Does life begin at conception?
- Does life begin when the foetus is actually born?
- Does life begin at viability?
- Is there some point in between?

Exam practice answer guidance at **www.therevisionbutton.co.uk/myrevisionnotes**

Mary Anne Warren lists the following characteristics of a person:

- Sentience – ability to feel pleasure and pain
- Reason – ability to think
- Communication
- Emotionality – ability to feel happy or upset and so on
- Self-awareness – ability to know oneself as different from others
- Moral agency – ability to be self-motivated.

She says it is not necessary to have all these characteristics – a foetus has none, but could be seen as a **potential** person, so killing a foetus could be regarded as murder as its future is destroyed.

Christians would consider a foetus as a person as it has a soul given by God. The precise time for **ensoulment** is debated – Aquinas thought it was at 40 days for a boy and at 90 days for a girl. Today, Catholics teach it is at conception.

Catholics teach that as it is impossible to say exactly when life begins, it is safer to say that it is from conception. Some say that life begins once the **primitive streak** appears (about 14–15 days), others would say it is at the quickening (the first movement felt by the mother, usually at about 14 weeks), others when the foetus has sentience (18–24 weeks) and others when the foetus has viability (can survive outside the womb) – with modern technology this is possibly as low as 22 weeks, the law says 24 weeks, and finally others such as Mary Anne Warren would argue for at birth itself.

Jonathan Glover argues that it is impossible to say exactly when life begins as a foetus is more of a person than an embryo and the Human Fertility and Embryology Act chose the fourteenth day for the last point at which an embryo can be used for experimentation as from this point single identity is established.

> **Potentiality** means that the foetus has a capacity for growth and will become a human person.
>
> **Ensoulment** is the moment when people believe the soul is given. Catholics believe this is at conception.
>
> **Primitive streak** is a groove that appears on the surface of the embryo which marks the beginning of the nervous system and individuality, which happens at two weeks after fertilisation.

Now test yourself

3 List Mary Anne Warren's characteristics of personhood.
4 When did Aquinas think ensoulment took place?

Answers on page 53

Tested

The concept of Quality of Life as applied to abortion

Revised

Questions to consider:

- What is a definition of Quality of Life? What makes a good quality of life? Who decides?
- Whose Quality of Life is more important – the mother's or the unborn child's?
- Does judging quality devalue the lives of the disabled?

The Quality of Life argument allows the value of life to vary according to factors such as pain, the ability to think and make rational choices. However, there is always the question of who judges this Quality of Life and whether that of the mother should take precedence. There is always the fear of 'playing God' and making decisions about a future life that we cannot possibly know. Peter Singer supports the Quality of Life argument by arguing for **replacement**: it is better to replace a less happy child with a happy one.

> **Replacement** theory is Singer's idea that parents should decide if a child they do not want, and who has few prospects of being adopted, should live. He says that those parents might replace it with a much healthier child, or they might give the thousands of pounds they would have spent on therapy and round-the-clock nursing care to UNICEF instead. He considers it to be heroic to save many healthy lives with possibly great futures, at the expense of one damaged one.

Problems with the Quality of Life argument

- The Quality of Life is subjective and has no clear definition – this applies both to the foetus and to the mother.

- If, when discussing abortion, Quality of Life is a consideration, how do we make decisions about what the unborn child may feel in the future?

- QUALYs (Quality of Life Adjusted Years) is a method used to decide if a life is worth saving if its quality will be poor. This is judged by professionals, so should Quality of Life decisions be left to them or is that just paternalistic?

Now test yourself | Tested

5 Who thought of the Replacement argument and what is it?

Answer on page 53

The question of rights applied to the foetus and the mother

Revised

Questions to consider:

- Do the woman's rights over her own body overrule the rights of the embryo/foetus?

- Does an embryo even have rights? Does a foetus have rights?

- Does Locke's principle of ownership of our bodies mean that a woman has property rights?

- Is a right always a moral good? So does the unborn child always have a right to life?

Potentiality is usually regarded as the best reason for judging whether a foetus has rights.

Locke's idea of ownership of our bodies comes from his idea of personhood – God has given humans rights over their own bodies, because he has given us the power of reason so that we can use it to improve our lives. Locke's ideas seem to suggest that a woman has the right to decide what happens to her body and supports abortion if it will improve her life and that of her family, as a foetus is no different to any other part of the body. To illustrate the idea of ownership of our bodies, Judith Jarvis Thomson used the story of a person who is kidnapped and plugged into a famous violinist so that their blood can be used to cleanse his blood, but it is only for nine months and if the person unplugs themselves they will kill the violinist!

For those who believe rights are an important consideration in the issue of abortion, the right of the foetus to life needs to be weighed up against the right of the woman to have an abortion.

Exam tip

When applying the ethical theories to the issues surrounding abortion you need to consider how they would approach the different issues NOT just abortion in general.

Application of ethical theories to abortion

Christian ethics

- The idea of Sanctity of Life is important to all Christians.
- A child is a gift of God and should not be destroyed.
- For Catholics, who hold a strong Sanctity of Life argument, abortion goes against Natural Law and is evil. They believe an embryo or foetus has the same status as any other human.
- Anglicans also see all human life as unique and intrinsically valuable so would consider abortion evil but they follow a weaker Sanctity of Life argument and so treat each situation with compassion.

Natural Law

- Preservation of life is paramount, so abortion is murder.
- The unborn child has the same status as any other life.
- The primary precept of reproduction must also be considered.

Utilitarianism

- Happiness versus pain is an important consideration for Utilitarians.
- Focuses on the outcome not the action.
- Life doesn't have intrinsic value for Utilitarians.
- Preference Utilitarianism considers the preference of mother, the harm to other family members and so on.
- Considers the foetus as a potential person not an actual person.

Kantian ethics

- Treat people as ends not means.
- Abortion could be seen as a right if a foetus is not considered to be a reasoning person.
- Abortion could be seen as wrong if the mother does it for selfish reasons only.
- Humans have intrinsic worth so this could be applied to potential humans too.

Exam practice

1 (a) Explain how belief in the Sanctity of Life may influence ethical approaches to abortion. **[25]**

(b) 'A foetus is not a person.' Discuss. **[10]**

2 (a) Explain how the ethics of the religion you have studied would approach the issues surrounding abortion. **[25]**

(b) 'Religious ethics fail to consider consequences.' Discuss. **[10]**

3 (a) Explain the strengths of Kant's theory of ethics. **[25]**

(b) 'Kant's theory of ethics is not a useful approach to abortion.' Discuss. **[10]**

4 (a) Explain how a moral relativist might approach the issues raised by abortion. **[25]**

(b) 'A relativist approach to the issues raised by abortion leads to wrong moral choices.' Discuss. **[10]**

5 (a) Explain how a follower of Natural Law might approach the issues surrounding abortion. **[25]**

(b) 'Natural law has no serious weaknesses.' Discuss. **[10]**

6 (a) Explain how the issue of personhood might influence ethical approaches to abortion. **[25]**

(b) 'The right to life is the most important issue when discussing abortion.' Discuss. **[10]**

Answer guidance online

Online

Summary

✔ The Sanctity of Life argument – Christian belief that all life is sacred – life begins at conception – only God can create and end a life – taking innocent life is intrinsically evil. However, the doctrine of double effect may allow abortion in some cases.

✔ The idea of personhood – not clear at which time personhood is conferred, it depends on when someone considers that life begins – the idea of a potential person – Mary Anne Warren's criteria of personhood – the definition of personhood is uncertain.

✔ The Quality of Life argument – this could be subjective – who decides? – is the Quality of Life of the foetus too far in the future to judge? – replacement theory.

✔ Rights of the mother and the foetus/embryo – does the foetus have a right to life? – do women have rights over their bodies? – do the rights of the mother outweigh those of the unborn child?

7 The right to a child

What is meant by rights?

Revised

Originally rights were seen to come from God – being made by God and being sacred gave us rights. Some still hold this view while others argue that our rights come from nature – simply because we are human and therefore have a higher intrinsic value than other creatures, and others argue that rights come from the duties or responsibilities that we have towards others.

A rights-based ethic can become individual as newborn babies have rights, but they do not owe any duties towards others.

Rights then are simply a result of being human and have an impact on every part of society, including whether a woman has the right to a child. This issue of right to a child raises many questions:

- Do all men and women have the right to a child?
- Do women of any age have the right to a child?
- Is a child a gift?
- Are all parents responsible enough to have a child?
- Who should pay for IVF?
- Is it right to use an unknown donor?
- Is having a child by artificial means playing God?

> **Typical mistake**
>
> Do not confuse the right *to* a child with the rights *of* a child or even the right *not to* have a child: abortion.

Fertility treatment and the ethical issues raised by it

Revised

There are many different fertility treatments such as:

- **IVF** – also known as creating 'test tube babies'.
- Surrogacy – where a woman is used as a substitute to give birth and then relinquish the baby to someone else.
- Artificial insemination – be it from the husband or a sperm donor.

Different health authorities have different guidelines about who is eligible, and at what age a couple can have fertility treatment – this leads to a postcode lottery. To fund it privately is very expensive.

> **IVF** is short for in vitro fertilisation. 'In vitro' means 'in glass'. IVF is the procedure by which sperm and eggs from the couple or donors are fertilised in a petri dish in a laboratory and then inserted into the woman.

In IVF, embryos are screened before implantation and only the strongest are implanted, in some cases imperfect embryos can be discarded and even embryos of a certain sex chosen.

The introduction of fertility treatment has meant that couples are less likely to think of adoption or fostering as a first option if they are unable to have children naturally.

Issues surrounding fertility treatment

Fertility treatment raises many ethical issues:

- Who has the right to fertility treatment? Can women of any age be treated? Do homosexual couples and single women have the right to fertility treatment?
- What are the ethical issues resulting from the procedure? What is the status of spare embryos and how are they kept or disposed of? When does an embryo become a person? What is the moral status of the donor? What about the cost to the NHS? What about the success rate of IVF? Is it morally right for a third party to be involved, whether as a donor or a surrogate? Is it morally right to pay a surrogate? Is it morally right to obtain sperm through masturbation?

Now test yourself

Tested

1 List some of the ethical issues surrounding the right to a child.

Answer on page 54

Exam tip

Exam questions usually centre round the issues surrounding the right to a child, NOT just the right to a child, so you need to read the question carefully and address the above issues.

Application of ethical theories to the right to a child

Revised

Christian ethics

Christian ethics would consider some of the following issues:

- Sanctity of Life – this is especially important if some of the embryos are used for foetal research or are simply disposed of if unwanted.
- The child as a gift of God – there are concerns about older women, and the development of saviour siblings. Some Christians do argue that women should have the same rights as men as far as becoming parents is concerned and age should not be a barrier. Other Christians say they should just accept their infertility as God did not intend them to have children.
- Possible adultery – the child should be the result of the love the couple have for each other and introducing a third party is almost like adultery.
- The sanctity of marriage – a child should be raised in the context of a heterosexual, permanent relationship between parents. This approach prohibits homosexual couples or single women from using sperm donors or surrogates to become parents. Some Christians do say that they should be given the same rights to be parents as heterosexual couples.

N.B. Fletcher's Situation Ethics would be in favour of fertility treatment in some cases – technologies and creative skills can be used for compassionate reasons and what matters is the outcome: the birth of a child.

Natural Law

- Any means other than natural conception would be rejected including the idea that masturbation to obtain sperm is wrong.
- Preservation of life and the belief that all life has equal status – the destruction of embryos goes against these primary precepts.
- Absolute theory – does not take into consideration the consequences of actions.

N.B. It could be argued that the doctrine of double effect is relevant as the creation of spare embryos could be seen as an unintended consequence of IVF.

Utilitarianism

- Utilitarians would weigh up the pleasure and pain involved.
- All actions are judged by consequences.
- The happiness of the greatest number would consider the cost to the health service and whether money could be better spent in life-saving operations.
- Preference Utilitarianism would consider that no one's happiness is more important than another's, so the happiness of couple is considered.
- Utilitarianism does not protect the status of the embryo, nor does it see it as sacred in any way.

Kantian ethics

- The Categorical Imperative demands that people are treated as ends not means. This would apply to the embryo if it is considered to be a person and to others involved, such as sperm/egg donors and surrogates.
- All humans should have the same moral treatment.
- There is the danger of treating the creation of human life as just another consumer good.
- Universalisation would question whether it is acceptable to offer IVF to every infertile couple.

Now test yourself

2 What reservations would Christian ethics have about IVF?

3 What would the response of Situation Ethics be to IVF?

4 Would a Utilitarian consider the embryo to have any special value?

Answers on page 54

Tested

Exam practice

1 (a) Explain the moral issues surrounding the right to a child. [25]

   (b) 'Having a child is a gift not a right.' Discuss. [10]

2 (a) Explain how a follower of Kantian ethics might approach issues surrounding the right to a child. [25]

   (b) 'The right to a child is an absolute right.' Discuss. [10]

Answer guidance online

Online

Summary

- ✔ IVF helps infertile couples to conceive.
- ✔ Embryos are screened before implantation.
- ✔ IVF can be seen as 'playing God'.
- ✔ IVF causes a problem with spare embryos.
- ✔ Older women, homosexual couples and single people can become parents – this raises ethical issues.
- ✔ Embryos can be treated as properties.
- ✔ The use of donors and surrogates can cause problems.
- ✔ IVF is expensive and the success rate is low for many couples.

8 Euthanasia

What is euthanasia?
Revised

Euthanasia is the ending of life because a person is in pain and suffering.

- Voluntary euthanasia is when a person's death happens *with* their consent without any coercion. Physician-assisted suicide is similar in that the doctor helps the patient but the final act is done by the patient themselves.
- Non-voluntary euthanasia is done *without* the consent of the patient, for example, if the patient is in a coma. There must be medical/family and sometimes legal agreement.
- Involuntary euthanasia is done *against* the wishes of the patient.

Killing or allowing to die?

- Active euthanasia is doing something to deliberately end a patient's life.
- Passive euthanasia is stopping doing something (such as when food/water is withdrawn) so the person eventually dies.

James Rachels says there is no difference between the two and passive euthanasia, although practised, is worse as death takes longer and there is more suffering.

> **Now test yourself**
>
> 1 What is the difference between passive and active euthanasia?
>
> **Answer on page 54**
>
> Tested

Ethical issues surrounding euthanasia
Revised

- Sanctity of Life – Christianity holds that all life is sacred which implies reverence and respect. However, there is strong and weak Sanctity of Life – what part does compassion play once the dying process has begun? Sanctity of Life applies to humans – is someone in a **Permanent Vegetative State** a human?
- Personhood – is someone in PVS still a person? How do we decide? If you are an 'incomplete' person, for example, you cannot move or talk does that mean euthanasia is acceptable?
- Many consider the Quality of Life argument to apply to euthanasia but who decides what this is or should be – the doctor/s, the patient, the family or a court?
- Autonomy – if people have the right to life, do we also have a right to death? Does right to life mean that others do not have a right to kill? But this does not seem to be absolute – what about wars, self-defence and capital punishment? It seems easier to justify killing someone who wants to die than killing someone in war who does not desire to die.

> **Permanent Vegetative State** or PVS is when there is no sign of activity in the brain and the person is reliant on artificial means to be kept alive. When someone is in this condition doctors may wish to end their life, but the family of the patient has to agree and usually they must be brain-stem dead.

> **Now test yourself**
>
> Tested
>
> 2 What are the main ethical issues surrounding euthanasia?
>
> **Answer on page 54**

Sanctity of Life and how it applies to euthanasia

Revised

According to the Bible, life is a gift from God and only he should take it away: 'The Lord gave and the Lord has taken away' (Job 1:21). This means that human life should always be protected.

The Sanctity of Life has been particularly important for Catholic ethical thinking about euthanasia. The problem today is that modern technology means that people can be kept physically alive, so Catholics now accept that there is no need to use **extraordinary means** to keep someone alive and the patient can refuse treatment when death is imminent – this approach sees the Quality of Life as important and takes a more proportionalist approach as people should not always be obliged to prolong life in every situation and that it is better to achieve a good death.

Euthanasia is seen as possible once the dying process has begun and life has in fact reached its end. The doctrine of double effect also follows this view as it allows the increase of pain relief knowing that a by-product of this will be to hasten death.

> **Extraordinary means** – according to Natural Law, moral duties only apply in ordinary situations. So a patient may refuse certain treatment on the grounds that it is an extraordinary situation and therefore is not essential to maintain life.

Personhood and how it applies to euthanasia

Revised

The problem with personhood and euthanasia occurs when a patient is in PVS. How do we decide how much consciousness they have? Many argue that using euthanasia on those in PVS, or those who cannot give consent will lead to a **slippery slope** and more patients would be killed, as what begins as a perfectly legitimate reason to assist a person's death will lead to killing people because someone else decides that their quality of life justifies ending it. They use the example of Hitler's rule in Germany as an example. Helge Kuhse objected to this as she said it was an argument from extremes.

Grisez and Boyle emphasise the importance of personhood and reject the view that someone can be bodily alive and yet not be a person – euthanasia they say is against the basic good of life.

> **Now test yourself**
>
> 3 Explain why the Sanctity of Life is particularly important when considering euthanasia.
>
> **Answer on page 54**
>
> Tested

> The **slippery slope** argument is when one moral law is broken and there is a fear that others will be gradually broken until no absolute laws remain.

Quality of Life and how it applies to euthanasia

Revised

Peter Singer argues that the worth of human life varies and depends on its quality. If the patient considers they have a low Quality of Life this justifies them taking their life or getting someone else to do it for them.

However, this again raises problems over who makes the decision if the patient is not able to and if this became commonplace it may harm the doctor/patient relationship. Is it allowing the doctor to 'play God' such as when they put DNR orders on patient's files without their express consent? This led to the guidelines on DNR orders being clearly restated in 2000 after a number of seemingly healthy patients discovered they had 'do not resuscitate' (DNR) orders written in their medical notes without consultation with them or their relatives. Additionally the Quality of Life is subjective and very hard to judge, so some patients may want to end their lives as they see themselves as a burden on others.

Autonomy and how it applies to euthanasia

According to John Locke a person has absolute rights over his or her body. John Stuart Mill (*On Liberty*) says that people should have full autonomy so long as it does not harm others. Many of those who support euthanasia believe that this personal autonomy is vital.

However, there is also the other side of the coin that autonomy gives people the right to life and so the right not to be killed: personal autonomy often conflicts with other values.

Useful case studies

Quality of Life:

- Daniel James was a young rugby player who was paralysed in a rugby scrum. He chose to die at Dignitas rather than lead a life as a paraplegic.
- Tony Nicklinson had locked-in syndrome after a stroke. He died after refusing food or treatment for pneumonia for a week following a rejection by the High Court of his case that doctors should be allowed to assist his death without facing prosecution.

Autonomy:

- Nan Maitland aged 84 chose to die at Dignitas rather than suffer a 'dwindling old age'.

> **Exam tip**
> Use pertinent case studies to back up your explanations and arguments.

Application of ethical theories to euthanasia

Christian ethics

- Christian views on euthanasia are linked to those on suicide – it is intrinsically wrong and rejecting God's gift of life.
- Euthanasia is against God's will and plan.
- The Sanctity of Life should be preserved.
- Situation Ethics may consider euthanasia to be the most loving thing in the circumstances. This does not consider the Quality of Life but stresses the need for agape.

Natural Law

- Euthanasia goes against the primary precept of the preservation of life.
- Taking life is intrinsically wrong.
- Nature should be allowed to take its own course without human intervention.
- Natural Law does allow a patient to refuse treatment – extraordinary means.
- The doctrine of double effect can be applied.

Utilitarianism

- Utilitarianism would look for the best consequence for the greatest number.
- It rejects the Sanctity of Life argument.

- Focuses on the Quality of Life argument – pleasure versus pain.
- Patients' interests are a minority and this means no protection against the majority.
- Mill would stress autonomy.

Kantian ethics

- People should not be treated as ends not means.
- The person has a moral duty to others such as family and doctors. Doctors have a duty of care to the patient which means that euthanasia is wrong as it would go against these duties.
- Any decisions should be made using reason and should be objective, unemotional decisions.
- Euthanasia is difficult to universalise, as Kant also thought personal autonomy and freedom were important.

Now test yourself

Tested

4 Would Utilitarianism support euthanasia?
5 What problems would a Utilitarian face when considering the ethical issues surrounding euthanasia?

Answers on page 54

Exam practice

1 (a) Explain Natural Law theory. [25]
  (b) 'Natural Law is not the best approach to euthanasia.' Discuss. [10]
2 (a) Explain how Bentham's version of Utilitarianism can be used to decide the right course of action. [25]
  (b) 'Utilitarianism is the best approach to euthanasia.' Discuss. [10]
3 (a) Explain why a follower of religious ethics might object to euthanasia. [25]
  (b) 'Human dignity does not matter to a follower of religious ethics.' Discuss. [10]
4 (a) Explain the main differences between Act and Rule Utilitarianism. [25]
  (b) To what extent is Utilitarianism a useful method of making decisions about euthanasia? [10]
5 (a) Explain the moral issues surrounding euthanasia. [25]
  (b) To what extent is the quality of life the least important factor when considering euthanasia? [10]

Answer guidance online

Online

Summary

- ✔ There are different types of euthanasia – active, passive, voluntary, involuntary.
- ✔ The difference between killing and letting die.
- ✔ PVS – issues of consent.
- ✔ Issues of Sanctity of Life.
- ✔ Issues of Quality of Life.
- ✔ Issues of personhood and autonomy.
- ✔ Is the maintenance of life an absolute?
- ✔ Is the act itself wrong or do the consequences make it wrong?

9 Genetic engineering

What is genetic engineering?

Revised

Genes are the basic building blocks of life, the blueprint for each living organism. It is possible to extract a single gene in a laboratory and manipulate that gene before replacing it in the cell it came from. It is also possible to put a gene into a different living organism.

Genetic engineering is the process of artificially manipulating genes.

Ethical issues surrounding human embryo research

Revised

- Sanctity of Life – using embryonic stem cells for research destroys the embryo. The law sets a fourteen-day (before the primitive streak appears) limit for research.
- **Therapeutic cloning** and **reproductive cloning** have led to fears of 'designer babies'.
- Genetic selection to remove genetically inherited disease.
- The boundary between natural and artificial becomes blurred.
- The nature of parenthood is adjusted, allowing parents to exercise control over the process of procreation.
- Does this take a reductionist view of humanity? Is a human nothing more than a lump of cells or a genetic sequence?
- It could help prevent infertility.

> **Therapeutic cloning** is a method of producing stem cells to treat diseases.
>
> **Reproductive cloning** is cloning that makes a duplicate copy of another organism. In 1996 scientists successfully cloned the first mammal – Dolly the sheep.

Ethical issues surrounding genetically engineered crops

Revised

Are genetically engineered crops good **stewardship** or interfering with God's creation?

Consumers are generally sceptical about buying **GM foods**. This could be due to health concerns or they might find it ethically dubious, so many supermarkets in the UK do not stock GM products.

Therefore, advances in GM foods may not continue, because if there is no market for the food, companies will not be able to afford to produce it.

Environmental concerns lie with the risk of production of 'super weeds'. These arise when insects carry pollen from a GM plant with weed killer resistance, to a weed. The insect population could be harmed and the weed could develop resistance to weed killer and grow uncontrollably; thus, disrupting the natural biodiversity of the area. At least ten genetically engineered crop plants are known to be capable of transferring their genetic qualities to wild plants and this could create serious problems.

> **Stewardship** is the idea of humans as caretakers of the natural world, looking after it for God.
>
> **GM foods** means genetically modified foods. They may be modified to be resistant to certain diseases or pests or to suit certain growing conditions.

Plants and animals can be enhanced to make them grow to a larger size, resulting in an increase in produce for farmers to sell and make a profit from.

Genetic engineering can reduce the need for chemicals such as pesticides, by creating crops that are pest resistant. This is cheaper for farmers because they do not have to buy spray for their fields and will increase their yield. Crops can also be engineered to contain resistance to weed killer; therefore, a whole plantation can be sprayed with weed killer and the crops remain unaffected. Reducing the use of pesticides means that they will not be able to build up in ecosystems and herbivores won't actually be killed; this can prevent the breakdown of food webs.

It is possible that the technology could be used to alleviate world hunger, growing crops in previously arid areas and increasing yield. However, poor farmers may buy seed they cannot re-grow next year and countries that are lent money for GM seed may find that their debt levels increase and they struggle to become self-sufficient.

> **Typical mistake**
>
> In examination answers, be careful not to see genetic engineering as all 'good' or as all 'bad' – try to write balanced answers.

Now test yourself

Tested ☐

1 How could genetic engineering be used to alleviate world hunger?
2 What are the problems with using genetic engineering to alleviate world hunger?

Answers on page 54

Ethical issues surrounding genetically engineered animals

Revised ☐

- Genetic engineering is often said to be no different from selective breeding and will aim to produce better quality food.
- Possibility of cruelty to animals because of the problems with cloning, as animals die young and have health problems. Ninety per cent of clones fail due to abnormalities or miscarriage.
- Fears of 'playing God' by experimenting on animals, and even creating animals specifically for helping humans.
- Genetic engineering on animals for aesthetic reasons such as fish that glow in the dark or for economic reasons such as featherless chickens.

Ethical issues surrounding human genetic engineering

- Genetic screening and PGD (pre-implantation genetic diagnosis) prevents genetic disorders being passed on to the next generation. This, as it relies on IVF, has a high failure rate.

- Issues are raised about the Sanctity of Life – in the UK you can only design a baby for medical reasons, but this will still involve the destruction of unwanted embryos. Also, what about 'saviour siblings' – is having a child just to save the life of another one fair on that child?

- Are we on a 'slippery slope'? Is this using the baby as a commodity?

- What about those who aren't 'genetically perfect'? It raises issues about equality and only valuing 'perfect' people.

- Fears that we are 'playing God' and taking charge of our own evolution by changing our genetic make-up.

The benefits and potential benefits of genetic engineering are vast. The most prominent benefit has come from gene therapy. Gene therapy is the treatment of genetic diseases by inserting healthy genes into a sufferer's 'dysfunctional' DNA. But if genetic engineering is used wrongly in humans it could interfere with evolution and change the entire human race for ever.

Exam tip

Genetic engineering is a vast subject so when answering an examination question just focus on a couple of areas, such as GM crops and genetic screening. By choosing to focus on two areas that pose different ethical issues you will have something to discuss.

Now test yourself

Tested

3 What could be the consequences of human genetic engineering?

Answer on page 54

Application of ethical theories to genetic engineering

Christian ethics

- The Sanctity of Life – human life, including embryonic life, has intrinsic value so should be protected.

- For Christians following a Natural Law approach to ethics, the modification of plants and using animals is considered to present no ethical problems.

- Using our God-given intelligence is good, but not at the expense of human life.

- Situation Ethics would apply agape but it's difficult to apply this to creating embryos for stem cell research.

- Genetic engineering could be good stewardship and being co-creators with God.

Natural Law

- The primary precept of preservation of life means using and destroying embryos for research is wrong.

- The use of adult stem cells could be justified as it preserves life by curing disease.

- Each human has value – regardless of any genetic imperfection.

Utilitarianism

- Prevention and curing of disease is fulfilling the greatest good for the greatest number.
- The life of an embryo has no intrinsic value.
- The pleasures brought about by possible cures far outweigh the cost to the embryos.
- The consequences are as yet uncertain as genetic engineering is still in its infancy, so the likelihood of success and the cost also need to be considered.

Kantian ethics

- Humans as ends in themselves – is the embryo a human?
- Could involve the exploitation of people – farmers for GM crops, saviour siblings, designer babies and so on.
- Universalisation – a rational person would choose to be born without a genetic defect and this can be universalised.
- Autonomy – human rights need to be respected, consent should be obtained.

Now test yourself

Tested ☐

4 Is Christian ethics against all genetic engineering?

Answer on page 54

Exam practice

1 **(a)** Explain the differences between the Hypothetical and the Categorical Imperatives. [25]
   (b) How useful is Kant's theory when considering embryo research? [10]
2 **(a)** Explain the main ethical principles of the religion you have studied with regard to genetic engineering. [25]
   (b) 'Religious ethics prevents progress in genetic engineering.' Discuss. [10]
3 **(a)** Explain how a follower of Natural Law might respond to issues raised by genetic engineering. [25]
   (b) 'All genetic engineering is ethically justified.' Discuss. [10]
4 **(a)** Explain the strengths of Natural Law theory. [25]
   (b) To what extent can a follower of Natural Law accept embryo research? [10]
5 **(a)** Explain how Utilitarianism might be applied to embryo research. [25]
   (b) To what extent can embryo research be justified? [10]

Answer guidance online

Online ☐

Summary

The issues surrounding genetic engineering and embryo research are:

- ✔ Sanctity of Life
- ✔ Medical cures
- ✔ Change in attitude to life and reproduction – saviour siblings and designer babies
- ✔ Using people as a means to an end
- ✔ Issues of universalisation
- ✔ 'Playing God' and interfering with nature, becoming architects of our own evolution
- ✔ Being good stewards and co-creators or just having dominion to do whatever we want.

10 War and peace

There are three main Christian and ethical approaches to the issues surrounding war and peace:

- Just War theory – there can be a moral justification for war if certain criteria are met and followed.
- Pacifism – war is always wrong.
- Realism – ethics has nothing to do with war and war is sometimes necessary.

Now test yourself   Tested ☐

1 What are the Christian approaches to war?

Answer on page 54

The principles of Just War and its application   Revised ☐

Just War theory is an attempt to give conditions for when war is acceptable and how it should be fought. Early Christians followed Jesus' teachings, such as 'love your enemies,' and followed a pacifist stance, but this changed when the Roman emperor Constantine became Christian and this led to the beginnings of the idea of a Just War theory as we know it today. The main architects of Just War theory were Augustine and Aquinas with later editions, meaning that the theory was always evolving to suit the times.

The Just War theory has three parts:

1 Jus ad bellum – when it is right to fight.
2 Jus in bello – how war should be fought.
3 Jus post bellum – how the war should be ended.

Jus ad bellum

All six of these criteria must be fulfilled for any declaration of war to be just. They are a mixture of deontological and teleological requirements.

1 Just authority – a war can only be started by a legitimate authority. This used to be the emperor or the king but today this is more complicated and the Catholic bishops in the twentieth century said that it should be a 'competent authority', which rules out wars started by corrupt governments.

2 Just cause – there must be a good reason for going to war such as self-defence or defence of another country, such as Britain going to war following the invasion of Poland by Germany in 1939. This rules out retribution. The problem with this is that every state that starts a war thinks that it has just cause.

3 Just intention – this must be as Aquinas said 'to promote good and avoid evil'. For Augustine it was in order to achieve peace and restore justice. The problem with this is that it can be seen as very subjective.

Fransisco Suarez (sixteenth century) and Francisco de Vittoria (seventeenth century) added three more:

4 Last resort – war can only be started when all other means of resolving the conflict have been tried, for example, through diplomacy (talking) or sanctions.

5 There has to be a reasonable chance of success – it is immoral to enter into a hopeless war. However, this is sometimes only possible to assess in hindsight, for example, the Vietnam War.

6 Proportionality – the benefits of waging war and causing death and suffering must be proportionate to the injustice that led to the war in the first place. For example, it would be disproportionate to go to war over fishing rights.

Jus in bello

This is even more important in modern-day warfare when civilian casualties are commonplace.

1 Proportionality – the methods used by the armies must be proportionate to the reason for war. This means that the commanders need to look at the suffering caused by their decisions and not just the immediate consequences. For example, weapons of mass destruction are against proportionality because of the long-term consequences to both people and the environment.

2 Discrimination and non-combatant immunity – innocent civilians should not be targeted. This rules out blanket bombing such as that of Dresden in the Second World War, and demands that prisoners of war be treated fairly as they are no longer combatants. However, this is difficult to enforce in modern-day warfare – landmines often kill or mutilate children, bombing is bound to kill and harm civilians as well as soldiers.

3 Obey international rules on weapons – this includes nuclear, chemical and biological weapons, but also methods of warfare that are evil in themselves such as mass rape or genocide.

Jus post bellum

This helps the move from war to peace and if used correctly should lead to fewer wars.

1 Proportionality – the peace treaty should not try to humiliate the defeated state so that it might try to seek revenge in the future.

2 Discrimination – civilians should be protected which rules out economic sanctions after the war.

3 Punishment – only those directly responsible for the conflict should be punished and this includes soldiers from both sides. Any involved in human rights violations should face international war crimes tribunals.

4 Compensation – the infrastructure of the defeated country should be repaired.

5 Rehabilitation – an aggressive or unjust government should be reformed.

Jus post bellum takes time and cannot be achieved quickly as the current situation in Iraq shows, but it can succeed as it has in Germany and Japan.

Evaluating Just War theory

- It gives clear moral rules for going to war, using the ideas of thinkers over many centuries.
- It is a flexible theory and changes with the requirements of the time.
- It allows the defence of the innocent and can thereby save lives.
- It is a universal theory.
- Many of the criteria are ambiguous and difficult to apply in practice. All wars involve the death of civilians (often called collateral damage).
- Many wars are only considered just or unjust in hindsight.
- It does not work against terrorism which seems to be the most modern way of waging war.

Now test yourself

Tested

2   What are the three parts of Just War theory?

Answer on page 54

The theories of ethical and religious pacifism

Not all pacifists are religious believers. Pacifism can be secular – many atheists, such as Bertrand Russell, are pacifists and take an ethical stance against war and violence.

Pacifists reject all violence and war but there are different types of pacifism; religious and ethical pacifists can be found in all types:

- Absolute pacifism – it is never right to kill another person whatever the circumstances. Some religious pacifists are absolute pacifists and follow Jesus' teaching such as 'love your enemies' and 'turn the other cheek'. One particular group of Christians that oppose all war is the Quakers. Important absolute pacifists include Martin Luther King Jr (a Baptist believer in non-violent direct action), Thomas Merton (a Catholic monk) and Walter Wink (a mainstream Protestant). This shows that pacifists can be found in all Christian denominations, although the majority of Christians would support Just War theory.

- Contingent pacifism – all wars involve killing the innocent and this is morally unjustifiable. Contingent pacifists accept wars in some circumstances such as self-defence and defence of the innocent, but at the same time the innocent must be protected. They will say that sometimes war is the lesser of two evils. An example is Bertrand Russell who was imprisoned as a conscientious objector in 1916 but believed the Second World War was justified to get rid of Hitler and Nazism. This view is basically Utilitarian.

- Preferential pacifism – this position prefers peace to violence as wars are so destructive but will allow violence to promote justice and peace. They will say it is sometimes immoral to take a pacifist stance. An example is Dietrich Bonhoeffer, who was a pacifist who took part in a failed attempt to assassinate Hitler to try to bring the Second World War to an end. He was hanged for his involvement in the plot.

Principle of Utility – this is often known as the greatest happiness principle. It is about the greatest good for the greatest number.

Proportionalism – an action can be right if there is a proportional reason to break an established law. In other words, a proportionalist maintains that there are basic moral laws which can be broken in extreme circumstances.

Qualitative – the quality of something rather than the amount of it. Mill looks at the quality of the pleasure not how much pleasure there is.

Quality of Life – the kind of life a person has or will have. It's related to the belief that human life is not valuable in itself (as the teaching of the Sanctity of Life believes) but is dependent on what kind of life it is and whether it is worth living.

Quantitative – something that can be measured. The Hedonic Calculus is quantitative, that is it measures how much pleasure is gained from an action.

Religious ethical theories – those that are based on religion and/or used by different denominations as a basis for their ethical teaching. Utilitarianism and Kantian ethics are not considered to be religious ethics.

Replacement theory – Singer's idea that parents should decide if a child they do not want, and who has few prospects of being adopted, should live. He says that those parents might replace it with a much healthier child, or they might give the thousands of pounds they would have spent on therapy and round-the-clock nursing care to UNICEF instead. He considers it to be heroic to save many healthy lives with possibly great futures, at the expense of one damaged one.

Reproductive cloning – cloning that makes a duplicate copy of another organism. In 1996 scientists successfully cloned the first mammal – Dolly the sheep.

Sanctity of Life – the teaching that all human life is sacred and special as we are made in God's image. The belief that human life is valuable in itself.

Secondary precepts – worked out from the primary precepts of Natural Law and are more flexible.

Slippery slope argument – this is when one moral law is broken and there is a fear that others will be gradually broken until no absolute laws remain.

Speciesism – giving moral preference to the interests of one's own species, over identical interests of members of a different species. Speciesism is an unjustified bias from Singer's perspective (similar to a racist or sexist bias in favour of the well-being of members of one's own race or sex).

Stewardship – the idea of humans as caretakers of the natural world, looking after it for God.

Summum bonum – the supreme good that we pursue through moral actions.

Synderesis Rule – we know the basic principles of morality and always intend to do good and avoid evil.

'Teleological' – from the Greek word '*telos*' which means end or purpose. Teleological ethics look at the consequences or result of an action to determine whether it is right or wrong.

Telos – the Greek word for purpose or end.

Therapeutic cloning – a method of producing stem cells to treat diseases.

Universalisation – a moral law which is obeyed at all times everywhere.

Virtue Ethics – this concerns habitually doing what is right. To be a good person requires practising virtuous behaviour.

Glossary

Absolute – universal and applying to everyone no matter what the situation.

Agape – from one of the Greek words meaning love – a love that is different from liking, familial love or erotic love. For Christians it means the unconditional love that must be shown to others.

Autonomy – self-rule: someone who makes moral decisions freely is said to be an autonomous moral agent.

Categorical Imperative – a command to perform actions that are absolute moral rules that do not consider consequences.

Christian Realism – the belief that Christians may use violence to bring about the Kingdom of God and secure peace on earth.

Deontological – from the Greek word '*deon*' meaning duty. When applied to ethics, deontological means that actions are right or wrong in themselves, regardless of the consequences. For example, it is wrong to torture captured soldiers even if you think you would get a good outcome such as vital information that might end the war more quickly.

Dependency thesis – morality depends on the nature of each individual culture.

Diversity thesis – morality varies as there is such diversity across and within cultures.

Doctrine of double effect – an action where the intention is good but may have bad side-effects. The good intention makes the action good.

Ensoulment – the moment when people believe the soul is given. Catholics believe this is at conception.

Duty – for Kant doing good means rationally determining and doing your duty. Duty is your motive for acting in a moral way.

Extraordinary means – according to Natural Law, moral duties only apply in ordinary situations. So a patient may refuse certain treatment on the grounds that it is an extraordinary situation and therefore is not essential to maintain life.

Free will – the God-given ability to make free decisions and choices.

GM foods – genetically modified foods. They may be modified to be resistant to certain diseases or pests or to suit certain growing conditions.

Golden Rule – the teaching of Jesus that we should treat others as we would like to be treated.

Good will – making a moral choice expresses a good will. It is the resolve to act in such a way that we fulfil our duty.

Hedonic Calculus – Bentham's way of measuring the good and bad effects of an action.

Hypothetical Imperative – an action that achieves some goal or end.

Impartial spectator – someone who does not count their own preferences as more important than the preferences of others. It is someone who can take an objective rather than a subjective view.

IVF – short for in vitro fertilisation. 'In vitro' means 'in glass'. IVF is the procedure by which sperm and eggs from the couple or donors are fertilised in a petri dish in a laboratory and then inserted into the woman.

Just War theory – a set of rules about when it is just to go to war, and just ways to fight and end a war.

Kingdom of ends – in Kantian ethics this means a world in which people do not treat others as means but only as ends.

Maxims – general rules or laws.

Objectively – this means that if something is right or wrong, it is right or wrong irrespective of one's individual or cultural viewpoint – it is absolutely right or wrong.

Omnibenevolent – a term applied to the God of classical theism, meaning that God is all-good.

Pacifism – the belief that acts of violence are always wrong. A follower of pacifism is called a pacifist.

Permanent Vegetative State or PVS – when there is no sign of activity in the brain and the person is reliant on artificial means to be kept alive. When someone is in this condition doctors may wish to end their life, but the family of the patient has to agree and usually they must be brain-stem dead.

Personhood – a definition of a human being as a person: having consciousness, self-awareness, ability to reason and self-sufficiency.

Potentiality – the foetus has a capacity for growth and will become a human person.

Primary precepts – the fundamental principles of Natural Law.

Primitive streak – a groove that appears on the surface of the embryo which marks the beginning of the nervous system and individuality, which happens at two weeks after fertilisation.

Chapter 7

1 You could include: the suitability of the parents, the age/sexuality of the woman/couple, the question of spare embryos, the cost to the NHS and the success rate, the involvement of a third party, masturbation, payment of surrogate.

   In the exam you are not required to cover every issue in detail.

2 Christians would consider the Sanctity of Life as applied to the embryo (disposal, use for research and so on); children as a gift from God and questions of older women becoming mothers; the introduction of a third party into the relationship and homosexual and single people becoming parents.

3 Fletcher's Situation Ethics would be in favour in some cases – technologies and creative skills can be used for compassionate reasons and what matters is the outcome: the birth of a child.

4 No, Utilitarianism does not protect the status of the embryo.

Chapter 8

1 Active euthanasia is doing something which deliberately ends a patient's life. Passive euthanasia is not doing something to keep someone alive.

   James Rachels says there is no difference between the two and passive euthanasia, although practised, is worse as death takes longer and there is more suffering.

2 Sanctity of Life, personhood, Quality of Life, autonomy.

3 Biblical basis, Natural Law, taking life is intrinsically wrong.

4 It would depend on achieving the greatest good for the greatest number. A Utilitarian would not consider the Sanctity of Life and would give greater emphasis to the Quality of Life and autonomy arguments.

5 The Quality of Life is subjective, the future consequences are unknown, for example, relatives may feel guilty, 'playing God', slippery slope, no protection for the minority, autonomy would dominate over other goods.

Chapter 9

1 GM crops eliminate pests and diseases in crops, enable crops to grow in inhospitable places, improve shelf-life, taste and so on, so more food could be produced which means there is more to go round, farmers earn more money to buy other food.

2 Disease resistance can make weeds pesticide resistant, cross-pollination, public distrust, reliance on multi-nationals, as the seeds are infertile and cannot be kept for another year, possibility of debt in poorer countries paying for the technology.

3 Inherited genetic diseases could be eliminated, Sanctity of Life could be ignored, change of attitude to human suffering or creation of a genetically superior people who can pay to be 'improved', parents having the right to choose their child, babies conceived as a means to an end, for example, saviour siblings, humans taking charge of their own evolution.

4 No, but Christians would consider the Sanctity of Life, the growth, use and misuse of knowledge, the most loving thing to do, the importance of stewardship and so on.

Chapter 10

1 Biblical teachings, Just War theory, Christian Realism, pacifism.

2 Jus ad bellum – when it is right to fight. Jus in bello – how war should be fought. Jus post bellum – how the war should be ended.

3 It is difficult to sustain in a world of non-pacifists and it does not allow the defence of the innocent as Elizabeth Anscombe argues. It can allow evil to flourish and dominate.

4 You could suggest the Quakers, Martin Luther King Jr, Thomas Merton or Walter Wink. Remember that although Gandhi was a pacifist and influenced Martin Luther King Jr, he was a Hindu not a Christian.

5 War is evil and the result of human sinfulness but it may be necessary to avoid greater evil and injustices.

6 The doctrine of double effect can be applied in war. For example, bombing a civilian area that contains an enemy command post – the intention is to destroy the command post not the civilians.

Now test yourself: answers

Chapter 1

1 God.

2 It is wrong in itself.

3 It could be arbitrary – God could say that murder it good.

4 It means that the source of morality is separate/above God.

5 When moral laws change according to culture, time, place and so on.

6 Check your answers against the list provided in evaluating relativism.

Chapter 2

1 Aristotle.

2 That we naturally seek good and avoid evil.

3 A real good conforms to Natural Law and fits the human ideal, whereas apparent goods are something we think is good but which does not fit the human ideal.

4 The primary precepts say what human reason says is right. They are the foundation of Natural Law and are absolute, applying to everyone without exception. They point us in the right direction to achieve human flourishing.

5 The primary precepts are:
- the preservation of life
- reproduction
- education and learning
- living peacefully in society
- worshipping God.

Chapter 3

1 Right or wrong in itself and stressing rules and duties.

2 Good will is the only thing which is good in itself. Goodness is in the will not in emotions, love or compassion.

3 Kant saw duty as using the will to obey the moral law. To act morally is to do our duty for duty's sake.

4 The Hypothetical Imperative is conditional. 'To achieve X I must do Y.' It is not deontological but teleological – it depends on the results.

5 Universal Law.
Treat others as ends in themselves not means to an end.
Live in a kingdom of ends.

Chapter 4

1 The greatest good for the greatest number.

2 Quantity or Quantitative.

3 Purity, Remoteness, Intensity, Certainty, Extent, Duration, Fecundity.

4 He said it gave equal value to all pleasures and it was swine philosophy. It emphasised pleasure alone. It did not respect minorities.

5 Quality or Qualitative.

6

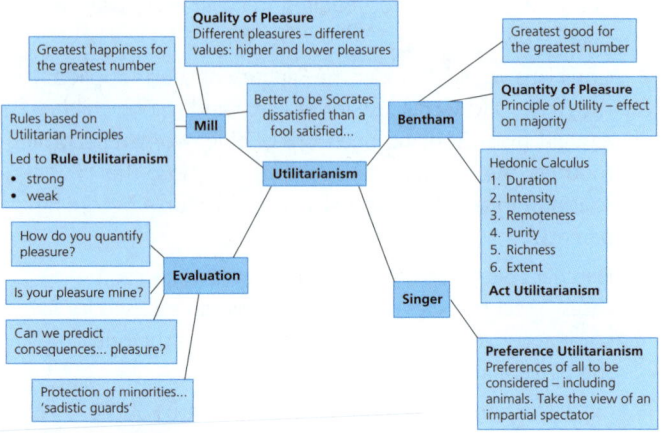

Chapter 5

1 No, some see it as the actual word of God to be followed absolutely, while others see it as inspired by God and in need of interpretation.

2 'Do to others as you would have them do to you' (Matthew 7:12).

3 Paul believed that God would soon come and establish his kingdom, but when this did not happen subsequent generations of Christians played a vital role in social reform.

4 This is teachings which come from the Pope and/or the bishops, mostly through encyclicals.

5 Agape or sacrificial love.

6 **1)** Pragmatism – the decision must work in practice.
2) Relativism – there are no fixed rules except agape.
3) Positivism – decisions are based on agape not reason.
4) Personalism – people come before rules and laws.

Chapter 6

1 The Sanctity of Life, personhood, the Quality of Life and the rights of the mother and the foetus.

2 The Sanctity of Life.

3
- Sentience – ability to feel pleasure and pain
- Reason – ability to think
- Communication
- Emotionality – ability to feel happy or upset and so on
- Self-awareness – ability to know oneself as different from others
- Moral agency – ability to be self-motivated.

4 At 40 days for a boy and at 90 days for a girl, but today Catholics teach that it occurs from conception.

5 Peter Singer. It is the argument that it is better to replace an unhappy child (for example, a disabled foetus) with a happy one.

Utilitarianism

- War is good if it produces good results – the loss of life and suffering have to be outweighed by the benefit.
- It is difficult to apply the Hedonic Calculus to war as there are too many uncertainties.
- Like Just War theory, Utilitarians would assess the likelihood of success – the ends must always justify the means.

Kantian ethics

- Applying the Categorical Imperative to issues surrounding war and peace is not simple.
- It is difficult to universalise killing and Kant would not allow killing for some greater good, nor would he allow people to be used as a means to an end. However, if going to war only in self-defence were universalised, then war would be eliminated.
- Kant does emphasise duty – this would include the duty of a soldier to defend his country and to protect the innocent, so conflict can sometimes change society for the better.
- Living in a kingdom of ends is reflected in *On Perpetual Peace* where he recommends a federation of states which forbade war – this was the forerunner of the League of Nations (1919–39) and then the United Nations.
- Kant's deontological ethics is sometimes teleological when it comes to war.

> **Exam tip**
>
> It is worth reading Kant's *On Perpetual Peace* which is quite short and gives a different perspective from the universalisation and stress on duty of the Categorical Imperative.

> **Now test yourself**
>
> 6 How can the doctrine of double effect be applied in war?
>
> **Answer on page 54**
>
> Tested

> **Exam tip**
>
> Read the following exam practice question carefully – note that question 3(a) is only asking you about going to war so there is no need to waste time writing about how the war should be fought and ended.

Exam practice

1 **(a)** Explain how religious ethics might be applied to issues of war and peace. [25]

   (b) 'A religious believer could never justify war.' Discuss. [10]

2 **(a)** Explain the theories of ethical and religious pacifism. [25]

   (b) Assess the claim that killing in war is more justifiable than other types of killing. [10]

3 **(a)** Explain how the followers of the religion you have studied justify going to war. [25]

   (b) 'Religious believers should be pacifist.' Discuss. [10]

4 **(a)** Explain Kant's ethical approach to war and peace. [25]

   (b) 'Kantian ethics offer little help when considering issues of war and peace.' Discuss. [10]

Answer guidance online

Online

Summary

- ✔ Just War theory looks at when it is right to fight, how war should be fought and how it should be ended.
- ✔ Just War theory is essentially Christian but can be followed by anyone as it is universal.
- ✔ Just War theory was added to by a variety of thinkers right up to the present day.
- ✔ Pacifism argues that Just War theory ignores the pacifist stance of Jesus and the early Christians.

- ✔ Pacifism opposes all forms of violence, but it is not necessary to be Christian to be a pacifist.
- ✔ There are three forms of pacifism: absolute, contingent and preferential.
- ✔ Christian Realism argues that states need to use force to maintain a just society.
- ✔ Realists say that moral rules that apply to individuals do not apply to states.

Evaluation of pacifism

Revised

- It is a clear-cut position with no ambiguity.
- It follows the teachings of Jesus and the stance of the early Christian Church.
- It supports the Sanctity of Life.
- It is difficult to sustain in a world of non-pacifists and it does not allow the defence of the innocent as Elizabeth Anscombe argues.
- It can allow evil to flourish and dominate.

Now test yourself

3 What are the arguments against pacifism?

4 Give two examples of Christian pacifists.

Answers on page 54

Tested

Realism

Revised

Realists say that war is non-moral – whereas killing is wrong for individuals there is no moral authority which tells nations how to act. A state simply needs to look after its own interests.

Christian Realism

Reinhold Neibuhr said that people are too sinful to achieve ethical ideals. War is evil and the result of human sinfulness but it may be necessary to avoid greater evil and injustices. Neibuhr thought war necessary to get rid of fascism and believed states, unlike individuals, needed to consider their own self-interest. This approach is known as **Christian Realism**.

> **Christian Realism** is the belief that Christians may use violence to bring about the Kingdom of God and secure peace on earth.

Now test yourself

5 What does a Christian Realist think about war and why do they think it is justified?

Answer on page 54

Tested

Application of ethical theories to war and peace

Revised

Christian ethics

- The Bible presents no single viewpoint on war and peace.
- The Old Testament shows both a revengeful God who destroys the enemies of his people and a God of peace.
- The New Testament says nothing about war between states, but many teachings, such as 'Blessed are the peacemakers' and 'love your enemies' seem to imply a pacifist position.
- The teaching about love and the desire to protect the innocent will lead most Christians to follow the Just War theory, but some will follow a pacifist approach.

> **Exam tip**
>
> Remember that there is not one Christian view about war and peace and your answer needs to reflect this.

Natural Law

- The primary precept of protecting innocent life will mean that a follower of Natural Law will follow the Just War theory.
- Natural Law would also consider the motives for going to war.
- War should be to promote peace and a harmonious society.
- Just War is Natural Law in practice in warfare.
- The doctrine of double effect can be applied in war, for example, bombing a civilian area that contains an enemy command post – the intention is to destroy the command post not the civilians.

> **Typical mistake**
>
> Candidates often forget that Aquinas is the architect of both Natural Law and Just War theory and think that Natural Law would oppose all killing, including killing in war.